# The Secret Language of Hypnotherapy

## by

## John Smale DHP B.A. (Hons)

## how to

## banish problems and

## achieve your goals.

Published in September 2008 by emp3books,
Kiln Workshops, Pilcot Road, Crookham Village,
Fleet, Hampshire, GU51 5RY, England

Previously published by Exposure Publishing 2006

©**John Smale 2006**

The author asserts then moral right to be identified as the
author of this work

ISBN-10: 0-9550736-2-6
ISBN-13: 978-0-9550736-2-5

All rights reserved. No part of this publication may be
reproduced, stored in a retrieval system, or transmitted,
in any form or by any means, electronic, mechanical,
photocopying, recording or otherwise without the prior
written consent of the author.

www.emp3books.com

**Dedicated to my past, present and future clients**

**\*\*\***

**and Maxine, my inspiration**

# CONTENTS

Introduction                                         1

1  Hypnotherapy                                      5

2  Secret Language of Breathing                     10

3  Breathing Exercises                              15

4  Secret Language of Posture                       21

5  Posture Exercises                                26

6  Secret Language of Language                      34

7  Language Exercises                               40

8  Coping With                                      45
   - panic
   - anxiety
   - stress
9  Phobias                                          51
   - public speaking
   - flying
   - spiders
   - snakes

10  Personal Problems                               66
   - anger
   - fertility
   - insomnia
   - confidence
   - impotence
   - premature ejaculation
   - jealousy

11  Stop Smoking                                     88

**[MORE OVERLEAF]**

12  **Stop Smoking Script**                        94

13  **Weight Control**                             107

14  **Weight Control Routine**                     134

15  **Two Stories Illustrating the Problems**      140

16  **Self Hypnosis**                              145

17  **How to Hypnotise**                           151

18  **An Explanation of Hypnosis**                 157

19  **Panic, Anxiety, Stress and Anger**           174

20  **Goal Achievement and Visualisation**         180

21  **Milton Erickson**                            184

22  **Parting Comments**                           195

23  **Further Help**                               196

# INTRODUCTION

AS YOU READ THIS BOOK YOU WILL LEARN the seemingly secret and hidden meanings of everyday words as used by expert hypnotherapists to smooth the progress of positive change and goal achievement.

By following the suggestions you will acquire knowledge of great significance in improving your life. Whether you want help with stopping smoking, beating panic attacks, losing weight, getting a pay rise or being able to ask somebody for a date, you will get much closer to achievement when you transform your language, body posture and breathing.

As you learn the secrets of the hidden values of words from this book so you will win the confidence to get what you want from life.

The secrets are contained in using our spoken, thinking and body posture correctly and that means learning about the words that can harm and those that can help. We tend to think in easy ways so words creep in that cause us to doubt ourselves.

Too often, the language we use to think and speak with brings about the opposite of what we want. Inappropriate words worm themselves into our thinking and maintain our fears, worries and habits. Even some trained hypnotherapists can use words so badly that they run the risk of causing problems to grow rather than diminish.

This book will show you how to use the languages of speech, thought and body posture to eliminate difficulties and to discover how to bring into play the ways of thinking that ensure you have a happy and successful life.

As well as factual meanings, words have emotional

meanings that are hidden. It is a different thing to love a person and to love chocolate. There is a huge distinction between hating work and hating your neighbour. Learning how to understand and to change the emotional value of words is vital for getting what you want.

For example, people who are nervous about taking a driving **test** or **exam** are worried about the sense of success or failure from their school days. When we can think of a driving test as a **demonstration** of an ability to drive, it becomes easier. After all, every person who is put forward for their driving 'test' has demonstrated to their instructors that they are able to drive safely. It is important to be able to recognise the different values that words have. When we change the language of our thoughts and our conversations with others, then we change the ways in which we live.

It is easy to demonstrate that thoughts have an effect on the body. One extreme example would be going up to an old lady and saying the most foul four letter word you can think of. **Please never do this**. With that one word, from a distance, you would change her heart rate, her blood pressure, her muscle tone (she would want to hit you or run away) and her blood flow as she blushed and so on and on. There is no magic in the word but the lady's body instantly changes. The lady has most likely heard the word before but she has a negative emotional reaction to it, and now you. Think of how she would describe you to her friends.

Another example is the story about an old practice in India where the discovery of a dishonest person was made by making a group of people hold some rice in their mouths for a few minutes. The offender was found to have dryer rice at the end. This was because fear causes dryness in the mouth. It reduces the flow of saliva. The mind had caused a bodily change because of emotion. When that reaction is applied to public

2

speaking, we can see how some people 'dry up' and others 'choke' on their words.

Psychosomatic illnesses are more common than we would think. The word, by the way, comes from 'psycho' meaning the mind and 'soma', meaning the body. So, if the mind can cause the symptoms of illness then the mind can get rid of them.

Perhaps this is one of the very early uses of hypnosis where the old shamans and medicine men would appear to remove bad spirits from a person's body and bring about relief. Perhaps the theatre of the event caused the necessary emotional change to give the expectation of cure. Hope is the antidote to worry. In the twenty first century, this is the explanation of the placebo effect where people seem to get better after taking a substance that has no medical value whatsoever. The mind is given hope and then works to bring about alleviation or recovery.

There is an old saying that is totally relevant to modern life:

*"There are only two causes of misery; having things that you do not want, and not having things that you do want."*

As a hypnotherapist I have found that when the causes of all the problems that I dealt with are summarised, then we have to deal with two fundamental survival systems, namely the fight-or-flight response that got us away from predators and our ability to store fat.

Both of those things are automatic. Fifty thousand years ago, the mind took over and helped us to live. We ran away from our predators and chased after our prey. We stored fat to keep us going through the winters. All of this happened without conscious thought. Those things were, and are, controlled by a part of the mind that still uses that almost unintelligible primeval language.

In modern times, we are still the servants of those systems and as they appear to be so far beyond our conscious control that we can feel powerless against them. However, when we learn how to communicate with our unconscious thoughts, when we learn their language, then we are able to succeed and to make ourselves happy by changing the direction of our minds. We can achieve our goals by positive actions and intentions.

Hypnotherapy gives us back self control. We can work with our minds to achieve what we want. A hypnotherapist is a person who helps to facilitate change. Rather than controlling people, he or she is a catalyst for transforming lives from awful to wonderful.

As stated above, the keys for improvements to problems will involve three elements; breathing, body posture and language. The book starts with guidance on how to work with those fundamental things. Please read those sections first and do the practice exercises.

It will then describe specific problems and how to eliminate them. The mind changes take place after you are shown how to use the techniques to eliminate your specific problem.

A quick note. I refer to the non conscious part of the mind as the unconscious rather than the subconscious in the book. It is simply my personal preference as a term.

# CHAPTER ONE

## HYPNOTHERAPY

*"There is no need for you to put up with something inside of yourself but outside of your control."*

HYPNOTHERAPY IS THE USE OF HYPNOSIS for therapy, to state the obvious. However, the approach has to vary with the problem presented. It is senseless to attempt to use the same techniques of suggestion therapy used for helping somebody to stop smoking with a victim of abuse. This requires a totally different approach to resolve the issues of the victim.

Equally, the techniques used by stage hypnotists to give the impression of power for entertainment would be totally ridiculous when dealing with clients who fear being controlled. Indeed, the vast majority of clients that I have seen have been controlled by their problems. A hypnotherapist works **with** clients rather than using people as tools for amusement.

Hypnotherapy is based on communication with the mind to bring about favourable change. Surprisingly, sometimes this is done without an apparent induction. It can happen by encouraging the client to reframe their problem by placing it in the past. Therefore, if a problem exists only in history, then the relief from the problem is in the current and future states. "I used to have problem xyz, but now, and in the future, I am free of that issue. I am something else other than I used to be. I am now without my old difficulties."

This is the principle by which a book is a valuable asset for the person who has problems. It will enable you to change the negatives in your mind to more positive views of yourself.

## So, what is hypnosis?

There is a huge mythology about hypnosis. Rather than being a state where people can be made to do things against their will as suggested by watching stage and TV hypnotists, clinical hypnosis used by therapists sets a frame of mind that may be influenced by beneficial suggestions.

When used correctly, hypnosis is totally safe. You never feel that you are in a 'trance', whatever that is supposed to be. Instead, a pleasant and deep level of relaxation is experienced.

The feeling resembles a light slumber. The word hypnosis came from the Greek word 'Hypnos ' (to sleep), but far from being asleep, the person experiencing hypnosis may feel a state of heightened attention, in which they still have overall control of their thoughts, whilst being distracted from the day to day issues that often interfere with clear thinking. Contrary to popular belief, the client is awake, aware and fully conscious.

## So what happens when I am hypnotised?

Whether the hypnosis is self-induced or applied by another person, everything that takes place is remembered clearly. When a person is in therapeutic hypnosis some basic things happen:

1. Memory is enhanced.

2. Acceptance of beneficial and positive suggestions is increased.

3. Other senses (hearing and smell) are much more acute, hence you will hear everything that goes on and everything that the therapist says.

4. The state of mind that is induced by the hypnotist is a very pleasurable, relaxing experience.

5. The awareness of time passing becomes distorted.

As a therapist, the one word that I avoid is 'trance'. It is emotionally charged and derives from the stage hypnotists, past and present. It implies power over somebody. The language used by the entertainer is 'to put somebody in a 'trance', as if it involves some sort of magic.

Hypnosis is based on the deep relaxation of the mind and body. Hypnotherapy is the use of that state of mind to bring about positive change.

Hypnotherapy techniques used by a therapist for change include:

**Regression**.

This is where a client is encouraged to remember an earlier stage in life. In this way, a client can recall when he/she was more able to cope. It is nothing to do with previous lives. I have no belief in previous lives, but I hope that is something after this one!

**Guided imagery.**

Is where the client is given a positive experience during which change can take place by visiting a different future in which problems have ceased to be. A common factor with people who are depressed is that they rarely see beyond the present. When somebody can visualise a future that is better than today, progress has been made. It is very similar to visualisation.

**Repetition, affirmations and visualisation.**

Suggestions are repeated over and over to bring about

the required changes. In doing this, the use of the appropriate language is vital. Affirmations are those positive suggestions that assert something to be true. They argue with the part of the mind that is causing negativity. And, when repeated often enough, they win.

By repeating positives and/or visualising them as outcomes, the mind accepts a new future. When affirmations are made then the mind believes the experience and reacts accordingly. For example, when a flying phobic sees himself on an aircraft enjoying the experience, then when he next flies the mind refers to the positive experience, although imagined, rather than the negative associations held in the past.

**Hypnoanalysis**

Is also used to help the client to remember when a trauma in his/her life occurred. When events are relived then they can also be put into a different emotional context for the client's current life. This process is easy to describe but often harrowing for the client. It should be conducted by an experienced and well trained therapist and, therefore it is beyond the scope of a self-help book.

**Post Hypnotic Suggestion.**

Suggestions are made that will continue to be active after the treatment session.

All of the above are methods by which the mind can be changed but there are methods that push away the natural systems we own that cause problems. These are described in the following chapters.

**So, how can a book hypnotise me?**

Hypnosis is no different to the state of mind that is obtained whilst daydreaming, reading a book, watching a film intensely or in meditation. There are no subjective feelings of being in a different state of consciousness.

That is why a book is beneficial. You learn techniques that will open the hitherto locked door to your unconscious mind.

The secret is being in the correct frame of mind. This happens when your breathing and body posture changes. You then use the correct words to communicate with your mind.

So we will now make a start on finding the hidden key to open your mind.

# CHAPTER TWO

## THE SECRET LANGUAGE OF BREATHING

### THE PRIMEVAL AIR-BAG

WE KNOW WHAT AN AIRBAG IS IN A CAR. When an emergency happens, the bag instantly inflates to protect us from injuries. Imagine that our survival mechanisms work in the same way. That is wonderful. It is how we managed to avoid poisonous snakes in our history. However, if the airbag in our car inflated every time we hit the brake then we would be prevented from driving normally or safely.

Our survival systems have become too much like that overactive bag. If, when we go to the supermarket, we react in the same way as if we were being chased by a tiger, then it is because our protection system has fired inappropriately. We need to fix it. The following will show you how to do just that.

### BREATHING

In history, breathing was considered to be such an important part of life that the word 'spirit' comes from 'spirare', the Latin verb 'to breathe', as in respiration. However, it is one of the things that is often overlooked, or misunderstood. The effect of the breath is at the very heart of problems and, happily, solutions.

Breathing in the correct way has been taught for centuries. To the Yogis of India the word 'prana' means the element to which all other substances might finally be reduced as is the spirit of life in Western culture. Regulation of the breath is known as 'pranayama' and it is practised for mental and physical wellbeing.

In China, the same thing is known as 'Chi', as in Tai Chi, a routine of slow meditative physical exercise for relaxation and balance and health. In other words, the practice of breathing correctly has been used for thousands of years for spiritual and bodily well-being. However, modern culture has dictated that we should have body shapes that emphasise the chest and minimize the stomach. That is the very shape that inhibits correct breathing.

We breathe from the moment that we are born so we feel that we know how to do it correctly. And we do. After all, we are alive! I get looks of surprise when I talk to clients about the correct ways to breathe.

The lungs are misunderstood! We tend to think of them as a pair of balloon-like bags in our chests that take oxygen in and push carbon dioxide out. They are, in fact, complex excretory organs. They are made from tubes and cavities that allow the exchange of gases. They remove many waste products as well as carbon dioxide, which is why we can smell garlic on people's breath. The little cavities, called alveoli, work constantly and are independent of the respiratory, or breathing, cycle. The process of gas exchange is dependent upon their concentrations. Waste gases either remain in the lungs until flushed out by breathing or are re-absorbed into the bloodstream when the concentration increases. The re-absorption of those exhaust gases can make people feel anxious, uncomfortable, nervous and irritable.

I remember visiting the tombs of the pharaohs in Egypt. There was no air-conditioning so the air became stale with the build up of the visitors' exhaled breath. It was surprising to see how many people were faint and dizzy. I witnessed seeing a number of anxiety attacks caused by those exhaust gases collecting in the depths of the tunnels. Rather than claustrophobia, I am sure that many of the problems were caused by the lack of fresh air and consequent shallow breathing.

As if to emphasise that point, I have met people who

have visited Aboriginal caves in Australia to view the paintings. These caves are air-conditioned to protect the art and there were no reports of problems with the viewers. What was the difference?

## THE BREATH OF LIFE

Sufferers from panic attacks are often told to take deep breaths to prevent hyperventilation. However, the instructions about how to do this are often very often counter-productive. Some experts appear to misunderstand what they instructing their patients to do!

We are taught from an early age that neatness is important in body posture. If you take a deep breath, as instructed by parents, schoolteachers and others whose intentions are to produce that neatness, then you will probably breathe into the high chest. This produces tension and stiffness in the neck and shoulder muscles, and a drawing in of the stomach.

If you simulate the position that you would adopt under attack, it is the same. The neck and shoulders tighten to protect the throat and the back of the head. The stomach muscles tighten to protect the soft organs of the abdomen, the liver, kidneys and spleen from injury.

In this way, advice to breathe deeply actually imitates the posture of somebody under threat. Remember that panic, anxiety, stress and anger are responses to a threat, whether real or imaginary.

It is important to learn to breathe deeply into the abdomen rather than the high chest. In this way you will signal to your mind that you are safe, and thereby evoke a recovery response that counters those feelings of anxiety.

Breathing involves two sets of muscles.

**The intercostal muscles.**

These extend downwards and connect the ribs. When they are contracted the ribs are pulled upwards and outwards to enlarge the rib cage (thoracic cavity). These are the breathing muscles that predominate during the anxiety state when the blood needs to be well oxygenated.

They can work rapidly to produce panting which can lead to hyperventilation where the blood is over oxygenated and leads to tingling in the extremities of the body and light-headedness. This accounts for the high number of panic attack victims who are admitted to the cardio-vascular units of hospitals.

**The diaphragm.**

This is a dome shaped muscle at the base of the lungs. When contracted it 'flattens' and causes air to flow into the lungs. Its effect is to enlarge the thoracic cavity in length. The diaphragm is the muscle that sucks air into the lower parts of the lungs and in turn, it flushes out waste gases that collect there. This type of breathing is indicative of a relaxed state. It is the natural way to breathe. Every child, including you, breathed in this way until school age.

Breathing, theoretically, includes the use of both sets of muscles to ensure an entrance of fresh air and the expulsion of waste products throughout the lungs. The high-chest breathing which occurs during anxiety states involves the use of the intercostal muscles and the locking of the diaphragm as a result of taught stomach muscles.

The exercises that follow will encourage you to use your diaphragm as the main muscle for respiration so that the recovery response, also referred to as the relaxation response, is evoked.

As we are conditioned to breathe with the high chest, concentrating on using the diaphragm will result in a balanced breathing practice. It takes some getting to but continue.

# CHAPTER THREE

## BREATHING EXERCISES

**NOTE. IF YOU HAVE MEDICAL PROBLEMS, SEEK ADVICE BEFORE DOING THE EXERCISES.**

HIGH-CHEST BREATHING INCREASES ANXIETY, as described above, especially when rapid. The breathing exercises that follow will help you to flush stale waste gases from your lungs and in turn, make you feel relaxed.

### 4x4 BREATHING

This needs a focus on maintaining the cycle. If necessary for comfort, change the duration of your count but ensure that the timings are equal for each of the four steps.

| | |
|---|---|
| **STARTING POSITION**<br><br>Lay on your back on the floor.<br>Place a medium sized book over your navel.<br>Ensure that your neck and shoulder muscles are loose and relaxed.<br>Relax your stomach muscles. | **START** |
| **STEP ONE**<br><br>Now, breathe deeply into your stomach to raise the book as if you are trying to lift it to touch the ceiling for the duration of a slow count of four. Check that your chest stays as still as possible.<br>(Please note: Whilst breathing in avoid inflating the upper parts of your lungs because they will fill automatically.) | **LIFT**<br>1...2...3...4 |

| STEP TWO | HOLD |
|---|---|
| Hold the book, in the raised position, for a count of four of the same duration as in step one. | 1...2...3...4 |
| STEP THREE | DOWN |
| Breathe out to lower the book for the same count of four. Imagine that you are lowering it to touch your backbone. | 1...2...3...4 |
| STEP FOUR | LEAVE ON BACKBONE |
| Leave your lungs feeling empty for a count of four. | 1...2...3...4 |

Continue steps ONE to FOUR for two to ten minutes twice per day.

The "4x4 breathing" exercise will slow your breathing down, thus reducing and eliminating hyperventilation. It also requires a great deal of concentration to continue. Whilst concentrating on breathing in a fairly unusual way, your mind will be distracted from the worries that caused you to be tense. The breathing, body posture and mental distraction make signals to your mind that you are safe from danger and the recovery response is brought into action.

This process makes you feel better. In addition, the act of relaxing your stomach muscles to enable slow deep-abdominal breathing signals to your mind that you are safe. This encourages the recovery response to relax you even further.

NOTE. This exercise is useful for helping with sleep problems. Lie on your back in bed, but omit the book.

One of the major keys to success in breathing for relaxation is to ensure that the muscles in your neck, shoulders, arms and hands are eased out.

The most important factor is to ensure that your stomach muscles are loose.

## STANDING AND SITTING VARIATIONS.

Deep abdominal breathing when standing or sitting is straightforward. Concentrate on loosening the stomach muscles. Stop worrying that you look fat! Breathe into your stomach whilst paying attention to your neck and shoulders. Let them droop. Do everything with your posture that you were told to avoid as a child. Let yourself relax.

When sitting, it helps to open your pelvis. Uncross your legs. Part them if it is possible.

## THE "I AM SAFE" TECHNIQUE:

Sit in a chair in a safe place.

Unfold your arms and place to the side, palms upwards.

Uncross your legs, open them and place your heels on the ground.

Become aware of your breathing. If rapid, slow it down consciously.

Relax your neck and shoulder muscles.

Allow your stomach muscles to relax.

Take a deep breath into the lower part of your lungs, allowing your stomach to expand. Remember that the upper chest will fill automatically so avoid filling your upper lungs. Hold this breath for a slow count of 4. As you slowly expel the air from your lungs, say to yourself, in your mind, the words: "I AM SAFE", and allow your whole body to relax, drooping your shoulders again as you do so.

Repeat this three more times, again saying the words "I AM SAFE" as you exhale.

When you have taken those 4 deep breaths, just allow the words "I AM SAFE" to drift around in your mind and allow your shoulders, neck and stomach muscles to really ease out and soften.

What the "I AM SAFE" technique promotes is the opposite of the reaction when threatened. The neck and shoulders are loosened, and the stomach slackened. This could be seen as an exposed position, but it signals to the mind that you are in a safe situation. Therefore, your mind perceives that there is no threat, and thus there is no need to start the 'fight or flight' response. Instead you enter the recovery state. This technique can also be used whilst standing, but keep your feet flat on the ground and your eyes open!

You may have recognised that this position is very similar to that adopted by practitioners of meditation, the difference being that the calves of your legs are stretched outwards rather than the legs being bent at the knees. Even the repetition of 'I AM SAFE' is like a mantra.

## CATS AND DOGS

Observe your pets. They know how to breathe because they do it naturally without regard to the fashionable appearance of their bodies. When relaxed and safe they use the diaphragm to breathe. When they are running you will notice rapid, high-chest breathing.

Say "walkies" to your sleeping dog and the

diaphragmatic breathing will immediately change to panting. Your dog is increasing the oxygen in its bloodstream to ready it for action.

It is a strange thought in many respects, but every animal on this planet breathes correctly apart from the human who lives in our modern culture. The desire for big chests and flat stomachs has caused modern society to adopt the breathing patterns that promote anxiety and stress disorders.

**EXASPERATION!**

When we are irritated by something, we often take a deep breath in, hold it and then breathe out with a sigh of exasperation. This is a natural phenomenon that, in our primeval days, took us from a high-energy state to a recovery state in brief moments. We can use this response without being irritated. It is similar in effect to the 'explosive relaxation' technique described later, but with a focus on breathing rather than posture.

The following is wonderful when something or someone annoys you and you want to overcome the desire to react aggressively:

Take a deep breath into the lower abdomen, then the upper chest. Clench your fists, become defensive. Now breathe out with a loud sigh of exasperation whilst loosening all your muscles including your hands and arms.

This is a naturally occurring defusing reaction that a parent makes when a child breaks or spills something.
**PHEW! THAT WAS CLOSE!**

We have all had a close encounter with something that was potentially dangerous such as a car swerving toward us, or an object falling close by.

We do the same thing as described in the 'exasperation' exercise. We move from a normal state to one of high anxiety down to recovery in a flash. Use this response to quickly take yourself from anxiety to peace.

Amending the 'exasperation' technique slightly; take a deep breath into the lower abdomen, then the upper chest. Clench your fists, become defensive.

Now breathe out with a release of that tension and shake your limbs gently. Then say 'Phew! That was close.' Now smile with relief.

## OPERA SINGERS AND SWIMMERS

An opera singer has to be able to sing long complicated word structures as well as high, low and long notes. Like a swimmer, the opera singer has to master breathing. Whereas it is difficult to imitate the swimmer's breathing patterns, it is easier to play a charade as an opera singer! Take your deep breaths and pretend to sing long notes. This helps you to automatically use both the intercostal and diaphragm muscles.

# CHAPTER FOUR

## SECRET LANGUAGE OF POSTURE

WHEN WE FEEL FEARFUL or aggressive, our bodies tighten. Just as there is communication between our minds and our bodies, there is interaction between our body positions and our emotions. When we adopt certain positions we tell our minds that there is a potential 'alert state', and our mental processes react accordingly. This is fairly obvious when it involves negative effects, but the body/mind relationship can be used in a positive way in order to mediate the fight or flight response.

**IMPORTANT**. Before you read on, 'Sit Up Straight'.

So! Did you sit up straight? No matter how you say or write it, that phrase will get a response. Even if you were speed-reading, it is likely that there was some movement as a total reaction or as micro-twitch in your muscles. Usually there is a reaction ranging from a slight fidget to sitting up as straight as a ramrod. It's a game you can play with friends and family! I did it when asked to speak about hypnotherapy to a large group of students. Even their teachers sat up.

Now, please sit up straight, and I am asking rather than telling. See what happens. You will notice that your stomach muscles and neck and shoulders tighten. This simulates the position we adopt when under threat.

Strangely, our culture wants us to be neat and tidy rather than relaxed. This conditioning starts with parents, school teachers and continues into adolescence where we come to believe that the classic 'V' shape is the most desirable. A big chest and a flat stomach are thought to be the secret of life by most people. Yet, the reality is that it is the cause of many problems, including adopting poor breathing habits. The shape is

21

promoted by fashion and cinema. Models, actors and actresses show the dimensions of a stressed human.

However, we are very similar to chimpanzees, gorillas and orang-utans, yet none of them stand to attention or sit up straight, apart from us humans. Only we have to eat with our elbows off the table!

Our body postures relate to our feelings of well-being. There are two phrases, which exemplify this connection between body attitude and state of mind, 'up-tight' and 'laid-back'.
When we are tense, nervous or anxious our bodies tighten up. This is because we are in the early stages of the fight or flight response. We feel under threat from something that is outside ourselves or from that feeling of dread that can grow from our minds. The closing up of our bodies protects us, to some extent, when under physical threat.

**UP-TIGHT**

This body position represents hiding from the environment, which includes people as well as animals and physical objects. We focus our vision into a stare (or close our eyes), tighten our muscles and protect ourselves.

When we sit in this 'up-tight' position our mind fears an attack and we become predisposed to anxiety or panic. The fear of anxiety or panic makes us even more tense, and so on.

This is the negative feedback-loop that we are breaking.

To feel how our muscles are linked when under attack, do the following. Relax your neck, shoulder and stomach muscles. Now tighten your stomach muscles. Notice how your neck and shoulders tighten in sympathy. You can do it the other way around. There is no direct connection between the muscles, but the signals from one part of your body are transmitted through your mind to the other. The same thing happens when you extend an arm and make a tight fist. The tension is felt all the way up to the neck.

When our bodies tense, our minds read the signs and start to worry about what the assumed threat might be. Think about the body positions of anxiety sufferers even when they are in a safe place. Likewise, the person who has been bullied will sink the head into the shoulders. The stomach muscles are firmed. The legs and arms are crossed. All without reason. We could understand the body posture if the victim were surrounded by thugs, but even when secure, the body reflects the possibility of being attacked. We can use the body to persuade the mind that there is no need to panic, that the best response is to relax and recover, to be 'laid-back'.

We are told that we have five senses; sight, hearing, touch, smell and taste. We actually have a real sixth sense, plus others.

The classic five senses are taste, smell, hearing, touch and sight. They are the senses that we use to monitor the outside world. We have others that monitor us. Things like balance and orientation. There is constant feed-back from our bodies to our minds through a largely ignored, but very important sense, that of **proprioception**, the awareness of the positions of parts of our bodies in relation to the rest of us. It is used as a preliminary drink-drive test by the American police.

To demonstrate it, extend the first finger on your right hand, extend your arm, close your eyes and then touch the end of your nose. None of the five senses were used until you made contact with your nose.

Now, without physically touching yourself, feel where your right hip is. Now feel where the sole of your left foot is. Now where your shoulders are. This body checking is going on all the time, but at a semi-conscious level. However, we can switch our conscious thought into it at will. This is the sense that will be used later to control your weight and also to help you to relax.

The significance of this awareness of body position and muscle tone in controlling anxiety is that when the body feels prepared for its assumed attack then the mind is involved and sets the fight or flight response into motion. Tension in the body promotes tension in the mind.

The contrary applies, however. When the body is relaxed, it signals to the mind that it is safe and the recovery response kicks in. We can consciously control the positions and tension of our muscles, therefore we actually have conscious control of the recovery response, albeit in an indirect way. We trick the system that is supposed to be beyond conscious control into action.

As written earlier, we are no more than primeval animals in modern dress. We still live in the pattern of our ancient ancestors. There are situations in our lives that remind us, at some level, of our earlier days and we respond accordingly.

In a society where food is fairly abundant it is difficult to imagine how we must have been when dividing the spoils of a hunt. Yet we watch hyenas and lions snarling at, and biting each other in wildlife documentaries on TV. We see animals fighting off rivals in the mating process. We were like that, so it will come as no surprise that we become tense and anxious in social situations that involve food and courtship.

I have seen many clients who used to be distressed in restaurants, or who were unable to swallow their meals. This unconscious worry about the possible aggression of others can lie at the heart of the panicking supermarket shopper where we 'take' self-service food, which we feel others want. It is different in a small store where we are served. Our ancestors would have felt comfortable when handed food, without risk, by the elders after they had first taken their fill.

We observe the bullying which takes place in schools as children play domination and submission roles. We see the worries that some people have in crowds where others are seen as unfriendly and frightening. The work situation is often difficult to cope with when colleagues and bosses are reflecting early social hostilities. Stress is more often caused by people in the workplace rather than by the work itself.

When we feel threats that are real or implied, then we close our bodies to protect our existence. Our muscles tighten and our minds race. This is the fight-or-flight response in action. Release the tension, open your body and signal your mind to calm down. When you do this, you relax because you stimulate the recovery response into action.

It is useful to watch pets when they are resting. They will sleep in a very exposed position when feeling safe and secure. Children, before being told how to sit like adults, will relax on the floor in front of the television. This is our natural and instinctive positioning until we are made to change to conform to adult standards of order. So copy children and pets. Learn from them. Lounge around and be casual. Then you will feel more relaxed. Be laid-back as described in the posture exercise chapter that follows.

# CHAPTER FIVE

## POSTURE EXERCISES

### EXPLOSIVE RELAXATION

THIS EXERCISE TEACHES YOU to recognise that instant relief is possible when you are feeling tense. Take up a tight position and suddenly explode into the exposed position shown in the 'BE LAID-BACK' frame below. All tension disperses instantly and you receive a sense of peace. Enhance this feeling with slow and deep abdominal breathing, described in the breathing section.

**BE LAID-BACK**

Expose yourself to the environment.

Signal to your mind that your body is safe from threat. Your mind will listen and bring the recovery response into play which allows you to relax even more.

This is the positive feedback that your mind and body need in order to find relief from panic, anxiety, stress and anger.

Here is how you do it:

1. Sit on an armchair or comfortable couch. Make sure it is sturdy enough to take your body weight when you flop backwards.

2. Tighten your muscles to adopt a rigid body position. Place the hands together palm to palm. Pull your feet back, close to the chair. Close your eyes.

3. Take a deep breath into your stomach and hold.

4. Count from 3 down to 1, and say to yourself, in your mind, the word "NOW." As you say this word, sprawl out. Your head goes back to the chair or couch. Your legs apart in front of you as make contact with the floor with your heels. Your arms fly out to the side, palms upwards. Now loosen every muscle until you look the same way as you did when, as a child, your mother said, "Sit up straight, you look like a bag of potatoes!"

5. As you slouch there, use one of the breathing techniques already described to enhance your feeling of relaxation. Breathe into your diaphragm. Imagine that you are breathing in and out through your navel!

Stay there for as long as you like, looking and feeling as if you are in a slumber, and enjoy the feeling. Repeat positive suggestions and affirmations to yourself.

The 'Explosive Relaxation' technique deliberately goes against those childhood instructions to sit up straight which is the position that you would adopt if about to be attacked.

In order to slouch, we have to slacken our muscles. In doing this we encourage deep breathing.

**SHAKE YOURSELF**

Stand in a safe place, become limp and gently shake your arms and hands. Slowly wobble your body and legs. Become soft and loose. Imitate the actions of a monkey. We are primates, so act like one. Act like a gorilla on traffic point duty.

**OPEN YOURSELF UP**

To use an ambiguous word, expose yourself. We are vulnerable on our neck, throat, shoulders, stomach and genitals. These are the parts that we automatically protect when under threat. So, to signal to our minds that we are safe, we can deliberately display those points of weakness with our clothes on.

Ensure that you are in a secure place and that it is appropriate. Sit or lay in the open position shown in the frame titled 'BE LAID-BACK', above. Loosen your muscles, breathe easily and deeply into your abdomen and allow the recovery response to work to settle you down.

## SMILE, PLEASE!

To demonstrate our body/mind relationship, force a smile for a slow count of five. Now do it again...and once more. Your mind feels less tense. You almost continue smiling without reason.

## LAUGH, PLEASE!

As with smiling, laughing encourages beneficial hormones to flow, making us feel happier. Laughing changes your mood as it helps you to breathe in a deeper way, hence 'belly-laugh'. Never feel foolish. The effort of pretending to laugh actually makes you laugh.

## YAWNING

Yawning is a natural stress buster. It causes you to stretch and simulates a smile with your wide-open mouth. It encourages deep breathing and gives an end point of muscular release with a sigh. It is easy to make yourself yawn by pretending to do so. Your body will take over on its own.

Remember, yawning is a precursor to sleep, the ultimate relaxation.

You have noticed that changing your body posture enables you to breathe in a deeper, slower and more efficient way.

## POSTURE HELP FOR SPECIFIC SITUATIONS

There are situational body postures, which promote feelings of panic, anxiety and anger. The following section describes some of them and gives help to enable you to cope.

**AVOID THE FOLLOWING:**

### 1. Ankle crossing.

When you are at work, commuting or when you eat in restaurants, watch other people. The vast majority will have their legs crossed at the ankles with their feet tucked back below their knees. This is a sign of tension. It causes the leg muscles to tense and this is fed back to their minds. Use your body to relax your mind by uncrossing your ankles and extending your feet forwards onto your heels. Breathe using your diaphragm.

### 2. Badly set-up computer keyboards.

If you use a keyboard or laptop, review the position that you adopt when typing. Very often, screen angles will cause the neck to bend backwards which duplicates the 'under threat' position. Some people in open plan offices feel vulnerable when they have their backs to their colleagues. Change your orientation if this is a problem.

### 3. Dehydration.

Dehydration, such as that which follows drinking alcohol or large quantities of coffee, makes people feel anxious.

Many people report having their first anxiety attack after drinking alcohol heavily during the previous evening. The solution is to avoid excess alcohol, to reduce coffee intake and/or to drink plenty of water.

## 4. Feeling trapped.

Feelings of being trapped are felt in a variety of situations including crowds, restaurants, cinemas, theatres, supermarkets, trains, aircraft and when driving. Treatments for specific phobias are given later in the book. However, the techniques for changing language, posture and breathing practices are key factors in controlling the fight or flight response that follows exposure to the situation or feared object. Tell yourself that you are in control.

## 5. Food competition.

This has a primeval connection. Food has been such an important factor of life since history began that we become competitive in any situation where there is social interaction involving food. This includes restaurants and self-service stores and supermarkets. Even the check-out, the place where some people feel like rushing away, is the point which represents losing the product of the hunt to scavengers. In these situations, remember that we are free of dissension over foodstuffs. There is plenty to go around. So much, in fact, that what we see on our plates or in our trolleys is always non-contentious, so we are safe.

## 6. Gripping.

There are specific situations where gripping an object can make people feel anxious. The tension of a vice-like grip tightens the muscles in the neck and shoulders. Then the stomach tenses and your body goes into an amber alert. From there, anything can happen! The common scenarios are the following:

- **the steering wheel.**
When driving, hold the steering wheel gently as if holding the wrists of a baby. You must maintain control, obviously, but without clenching.

- **the pram handle.**

Maintain control, but loosen your grip.

- **the supermarket trolley handle.**

If your load is heavy, a supermarket trolley can become difficult to control, so either shop more frequently, although this can become a nuisance and adds to anxiety. Better still, get your partner to push the trolley! Seriously, just loosen your grip.

- **the golf club.**

Gripping too tightly can cause enough tension to upset the swings of golfers. Another result is something called 'the yips', the inability to hit a putt on the green. If these are problems, loosen your grip, breathe with the diaphragm, and above all, just enjoy a game that is supposed to be a pleasure.

## 7. Holding a newspaper in the air.

As with a steering wheel, holding a newspaper can tighten the neck and shoulders, bringing about a feeling of anxiety. Look at the stressed faces of commuting business people. When they get to their offices, they are feeling either timid or aggressive.

When I wrote my first book about panic attacks in 2001, I wrote the following: "I believe that 'quality' newspapers should print in tabloid format in order to relieve their readers from the tension from reading broadsheets!" That has actually happened and I take no credit! However, people still hold newspapers in such a way that their shoulders tighten. Relax when you read.

## 8. Hunching.

Anxious people hunch in many different situations. These include meeting others socially, being interviewed, sitting in restaurants, driving, working and sitting at home.

Stand or sit without tightening the neck, shoulders and stomach. As well as looking more relaxed, you will feel it.

## 9. Sexual/Social competition.

This is another point of primeval worry. Anxiety, jealousy and anger come from the fear that we might be attacked or have our mate stolen from us. This is most easily seen in places where teenagers and singles meet. In these situations it is better to be with friends who offer security of numbers or to avoid places which have a reputation for trouble.

For mothers on a school run there is sometimes a worry about how others will regard their competence as mothers. You know that your child is the best in the world and that you are the person who raised him/her. Therefore you are the best mum, ever. Stop worrying.

## 10. Wearing a collar and tie too tightly.

Fashion works against us again.

The brain needs a large amount of blood flowing through it. If we wear ties too tightly, or if our collar is too small for our neck, then neckwear becomes a garrotte rather than clothing.

A tight collar will also put pressure on the neck muscles so that we tighten them to counteract the noose. This encourages our neck and shoulder muscles to contract which, as we know, stimulates anxiety.

Leave your tie off, or loosen it. If your boss is worried by that, get him or her to buy and read this book!

As a quick note. If you wondered what the 'secret language of hypnotherapy' has to do with breathing and posture, the first requisite for hypnosis is to encourage relaxation. The therapist will ask you to lie back on a couch or in an armchair and pay attention to deep breathing into the stomach. This is the secret language that involves something other than words. It communicates equally well and it has a vocabulary that is worth learning.

The next chapter deals with the spoken language, the bedrock of hypnosis and hypnotherapy.

# CHAPTER SIX

## SECRET LANGUAGE OF LANGUAGE

WHEN WE THINK, it is like having a conversation within our own minds. This is our internal dialogue. Those thoughts are 'flavoured' by our emotions. We run a process of risk evaluation at the same time. When we are walking we recognise ruts in the road, or dark corners where dangers might lurk. However, when we worry, we think about problems that might become reality without having rational justification.

We know that our thoughts can change our feelings. Fear is an emotion. Those fears that seem to come from nowhere have their origins in our unconscious thoughts rather than from a recognised stimulus. We react as if the threat were a real thing. Rather than thoughts they become 'feelings'. Yet when those thoughts are of pleasure, we relax.

The language that we use for our internal and external dialogue is important for our well-being and for dealing with the problems that underlie our anxiety. Within modern culture there are four things relating to language which work against us, but which we can use to our advantage when we know the secrets.

### 1. We live in a society that sells problems for a living.

Can you imagine taking your car to a showroom where you are told that the vehicle you have is perfect? No!

They might suggest that the mileage is high, or the engine size is unsuitable, or that the fuel consumption is uneconomical. They will identify and explain the 'problems' that you have and then they will solve them by selling you a new car. This applies to most trades.

Even salaries are paid because if your position were vacant, the company would have a problem in getting its necessary work done. We survive by solving problems, and then by maintaining the possibility of the problem recurring.

## 2. We use words too cheaply.

We sustain our personal problems by the poor use of language. That is, we use words too cheaply. We pepper our speech with brief idioms that communicate on a superficial level, but have different deep-seated meanings. My favourite example of poor language that is counter-productive came from a client who said: "Perhaps I really ought to try to think more positively!" That sentence contained all the reasons why she would find it difficult to do so.

The words 'perhaps', 'I really', 'ought' and 'try' are weak rather than positive. They are 'failure' words. They appear to state a positive objective but they infer that the goal will be missed. If the intention is firm then the sentence becomes, "I think positively."

## 3. We like negatives!

We tend to use strange constructions that are based on double negation. Why do we say, "that's not a bad idea" rather than "that's a good idea", for example?

Negatives are necessary for rational disciplines. Mathematics has to have the concept of negatives to work, but we are dealing with our emotions. As you will see later, negatives are unable to dismiss problems but they potentially intensify them.

## 4. We make our lives conditional.

We make statements to ourselves and then accept them as solid truths. Superstitions are a good example. "If I walk under a ladder then I will be unlucky" or "a black cat crossing my path is a good omen" or a bad one in some cultures! We make our lives conditional. If X happens then Y will follow.

This happens with anxiety states. "If I go to the supermarket then I will have a panic attack." I have even heard the statement, "I know that I will get a panic attack two and a half hours after taking my beta-blocker." Surprise, surprise! She did until we changed her language. Suggestions are quickly made and adhered to. When we make the wrong choices with suggestions then we pay the price.

## BREAKING OUT OF THINKING TRAPS

Our self-talk is full of traps. Most people have heard of the word **'affirmation'**, a positive phrase or suggestion aimed at changing the ways in which we think about ourselves. The most famous one is "Everyday, in every way, I am getting better and better." However, very few people actually use positive affirmations. Most of us are very adept at using negative ones by accident! We develop and hold onto erroneous beliefs that distort and change our behaviours and attitudes.

Sadly, we are wonderful in reinforcing negatives by our thinking. When we make negative suggestions to ourselves then we run a huge risk of believing them. Things like the following need to be ruthlessly destroyed. "I am unlucky", "I am ugly", "I am a loser", "I will get fired because I am useless at my job."

There is a way to break the negativity of our self-talk. We use very positive techniques for changing our language, which in turn modify our thinking, emotions and reactions. These are based on eliminating negative words and conditions. We replace them with a language and thinking that contains beneficial intention.

**The rules and steps are simple and easy to remember.**

Look at the sentence **'I will NOT panic** (or get angry/become anxious/get stressed, etc.) **in the supermarket'** (or in the car, at the restaurant, at work, on a date, etc.) This seems as if it will work.

However, within that short sentence there are three fundamental errors of thought that will bring about the opposite response. From working through this example, we see how to turn our goals into language that communicates the correct message to our minds.

**1. 'I WILL'** puts the hoped for solution into the future. The future is tomorrow, next week, next year, whatever. This tells us that whereas relief will be found, it is unlikely that it will help us <u>now</u>. Putting that hope into the future reinforces the problem that you currently have.

So the first rule and step is to place your problem into the past tense.

If it WAS a problem, then it follows that it has gone. Your mind gives you the unconscious positive suggestion, or affirmation, that you need. You put the solution into the present tense by using the words 'I' and 'NOW'.

The affirmation then becomes: 'I **used** to panic in the supermarket (or whatever) but **NOW, I feel peaceful, safe and relaxed.'**
If you find that your mind tells you that your problem still exists, then argue with it! Repeat your affirmation over and over.

**2.** The second rule is to lose the small word **'NOT'**. Although we know what positive suggestions are, we fail to use them. Instead, anxiety sufferers use negative suggestions accidentally. These maintain the problem rather than giving a solution. When we are thinking about behaviours, our minds seem to be unable to recognise negatives. When we use the word 'NOT' we often create the opposite outcome to that which is desired. Let me give an example: **'Do NOT think of blue elephants!'**

It is likely that you thought of blue elephants. It therefore follows that the sentence 'I will NOT panic in the supermarket' is understood as 'I WILL panic in the supermarket' because the instruction is contained after the word 'NOT' in the words 'panic in the supermarket'. The word 'not' has no effect in changing that instruction. The blue elephant example told you, after the word 'NOT', to **think of blue elephants.**

So, use a sentence that affirms what you want to happen rather than using a negative in an attempt to negate the unwanted effect. To repeat, lose the word 'NOT' from your thoughts. In its place, state the result that you want in positive terms.

**A quick note.** Whereas the word 'not' is to be avoided in suggestions and self talk dialogue, it is permitted in negating things as in 'blue is not green'.

**3.** The third rule, and next step, is to omit any reference to the problem when you are used to putting it into the past and when you have stopped using the word 'not'. The last part of the sentence is a reminder of the problem and it is emphasised. '...panic in the supermarket.' It tells you to do what you want to avoid. Never feed a problem by talking or thinking about it. Starve it to death. Make it an exile, something that used to cause upsets but which has now been eliminated. Eliminate the problem and tell yourself what you want to happen. 'In the supermarket (or in the car, at the restaurant, at work, on a date, etc.), I am calm, confident and in control.

## PUTTING IT ALL TOGETHER:

1. Make your suggestions positive, current and relevant to the solution. Ignore the problem completely. It is something that you used to have, but now you are fine.

2. Avoid certain other words such as 'perhaps', 'ought', 'should', 'maybe', 'if', 'might', 'probably' and 'try'. These imply either failure or weakness.

3. Make your internal dialogue strong and assertive. Tell yourself what you want to be by telling yourself that what you wanted in the future is how you actually are, now.

4. To summarise, model your suggestion on the following, "In the supermarket I am calm, peaceful and relaxed." Stop your language from telling you otherwise.

To end this chapter, can you see why 'DON'T PANIC' is the WORST thing to say in a crisis? 'STAY CALM AND RELAXED' is so much better.

The following exercises help you to change your thoughts to put your problems back into the past, which is where they belong.

# CHAPTER SEVEN

## LANGUAGE EXERCISES

THE FOLLOWING EXERCISES HELP you to recognise negatives in your inner and outer dialogues and give guidance in developing positive thinking patterns.

### Review your inner dialogue.

Write down your first thoughts about how you would like to feel. Now review what you have written and edit it to eliminate the words that affirm your problem. Rewrite your aims in positive words that contain the solution in the present tense. Check your words with the lists given a little later in this chapter.

### Become your own editor.

Editors check the constructions of words and grammar before publication. When you think, check how you are thinking. Your objective is to ensure that your thinking and spoken words are positive and direct. Delete any negatives that you find in your inner and outer dialogues.

### Two negatives do not make a positive!

Yes! I have used the 'not' word. As written above, using the word 'not' in a sentence with positive intent reverses the meaning. However, attempts to change a negative sentence into a positive one are ineffective. To demonstrate this, it is better to give an example. If we use the sentence "I will not stay calm" rather than "I will not panic" then they will both have the same effect of signalling alarm.

That little word is a negative influence whichever way you look at it! Throw it away. Refuse to use it. This becomes easier with time, I promise.

**Read, watch and listen to advertisements.**

Good advertising copywriters are skilled people who have to communicate messages which will evoke positive action. They sell the benefits of a product or service. You will notice the absence of weak words such as 'try', 'don't', 'won't'. However, notice the abundance of affirmative words such as 'will', 'can' and 'now'. Make sure that you analyse high quality advertisements. The most adept advertising professionals will have written these. Make a list of the active and optimistic words and add them to your vocabulary. Compare them to advertisements in local newspapers from small businesses. There you will spot the less effective use of language.

Some of you will be thinking that the word 'try' is used in advertising. 'Try our product and if you do not like it, get your money back.' This works on the idea that when you try something then the bother to get the money back will put people off making the effort. Here the word try invites people to test. It implies that the manufacturer has confidence. It probably has an effect. The manufacturer's risk is worth taking.

However, 'try to lose weight with our product' is different. Here the failure sense would be implied as happens in most cases of the use of the word. In short, lose the 'try' word!

**Listen to politicians.**

Politicians sell voters the apparent problems caused by their oppositions and then they offer the solutions that they think that they have. Watch news programmes to explore the language used. Notice the cryptic meanings of phrases such as 'their employment policy is not working', the hidden emphasis being on 'is not working' suggesting that there will be unemployment. The follow up would be 'our employment policy will bring rich rewards to our voters'. Remember that our culture sells solutions to problems that we create.

**Listen to positive people.**

Listen to the words and expressions of people who are confident. Their self-esteem is reflected in the language that they use with others. It follows that their internal dialogue is as assured as their outward speech. Copy them!

**WORDS, WORDS AND WORDS**

**Words to avoid**

• **Try**. Implies failure. Remember that when somebody says that they will try to see you at 3 o'clock, that gives you at least ten more minutes before they will actually arrive.
• **Not**. Creates a negative suggestion as alread mentioned.
• **But**. When used in the present tense to explain why something will fail. In this way, 'but' creates the negative reinforcement of the problem. For example "I would like to drive on motorways, but I panic."
• **Perhaps**. Conditional expectation of failure as in "perhaps I will get better".
• **Might**. Conditional expectation of failure as above.
• **Maybe**. Conditional expectation of failure as above.
• **Should**. Conditional expectation of failure as above.

**Words to use cautiously**

• All words which put action or intent into the future. They maintain the problem in the present time. However, if they reflect an intent that was previously missing and a time frame, they are useful. For example "I will go to the doctor tomorrow" or "I can relax when I visit the hairdresser in an hour's time."
• **Can**. A positive word that refers to the future but is

sometimes conditional.
- **Will**. A positive word that refers to the future.
- **If**. This makes the intent conditional. An example of bad usage is, "if I meet somebody new, then I will be anxious." An example of better usage is, "if I use positive language then I will be in control." However, it is best to say, "I use positive language and I am in control, now." (See below.)

**Words to use**
- (I) **Do**. A positive word in the present time.
- (I) **Am**. A positive word in the present time.
- **Now**. A positive word in the present time.
- **But** (when following placing the problem into the past tense.) Used this way, 'but' creates a positive affirmation. For example "I used to worry about driving on motorways, but now I feel calm, confident and in control."
- **Avoid**. This is a word of positive intent. "I used to get angry with myself, but now I avoid criticising myself by recognising my true value."
- **As.** A conditional word that implies a result. For example, as you read this book you find it is helping you to improve your life.

**FOLLOW THE RULES.**

Rather than just reading the language rules given above, become familiar with them, understand them and then adopt them.

They are:

1. Place your problem into the past tense and the positive outcome in the 'here-and-now'.

2. Lose the word 'not', and any other 'weak' words.

3. Then, omit any reference to the problem. Define the solution in 'strong' words.

As you change the language of your thoughts, then;

Your mind becomes more relaxed;

Then your body posture changes;

Then your breathing changes;

Then your life changes;

For the better.

# CHAPTER EIGHT

## COPING WITH PANIC, ANXIETY AND STRESS

### THE MIND/BODY RELATIONSHIP

THE MIND/BODY RELATIONSHIP is relevant and important in controlling those irrational fears that cause phobias, panic, anxiety, stress and anger. The mind appears to have total control of the body. We think that we experience the world through our conscious thoughts, which are moderated by our emotional moods. However, when we feel the crippling effects of anxiety related problems, the older part of our mind, the unconscious, takes over and we feel that we have lost all control.

Some parts of the body can be made to work with conscious thoughts. You are purposefully using your hands and eyes to read this book now. Yet, some parts of your body seem to be beyond conscious reach, such as your heart rhythm. Other bodily functions, like breathing, are controlled both consciously and subconsciously.

When we suffer from the crippling effects of phobias, panic, anxiety, stress and anger we are reacting to events and thoughts that create negative feedback. We feel out of control, we tighten our bodies and either hyperventilate or seem to stop breathing. These all seem to be beyond any control.

Yet we can learn how to create positive feedback-loops. In order to gain control of panic, anxiety, stress and anger, you change three areas of your life. This book will enable you to use language, body posture and breathing exercises to restrain and alleviate those feelings of panic, anxiety and stress.

## THE ADRENALINE RUSH

The adrenaline rush, referred to as the fight-or-flight response, is what causes the reaction of panic or anger, the 'red-alert' states. When it happens at a lower, or stand-by level, and over a period of time it becomes anxiety or stress, the 'amber' state. This response is what has kept humans alive for the past fifty thousand years even though it was, and is, expensive in terms of energy usage.

We are comparatively weak and we are soft bodied. We have no claws or fangs or armour but we have avoided extinction at the claws and teeth of much stronger creatures. Now we are strong because we have guns, knives and chemicals with which we dominate our adversaries. The need to run away from, or fight off a threat has become unnecessary. However, the response remains and is inappropriate most of the time.

Back in those primeval times, energy was expensive. When our ancestors were experiencing the fight-or-flight response they were burning up energy at a high rate. To replace it meant much more time spent in hunting or gathering. That high-energy state needed instant restoration to a low energy state, which is referred to in this book as the recovery response. Although in our modern age we can replace energy easily with readily available foods, the ability to rapidly evoke the recovery response is still with us, but we need to learn how to initiate it. We have to find the secret codes.

## FINDING HELP

Earlier, this book explained why language, posture and breathing are related to feelings of fear and how, when changed, they can be used to bring you control, peace and tranquillity.

Exercises for developing your controls were shown within each section for easier reference at those times when you need to find and use them quickly. Presumably, as you have bought this book, you want to get help as quickly as possible. To this end, information about the causes of the fight or flight response is shown in a separate chapter at the end. Read it at leisure after you have started to regain control.

Fear, anxiety and anger have been described as 'something deep inside over which we have no control'. The good news is that we do have the ways to take command of those feelings. All we need is the knowledge for using them.

## PANIC ATTACKS, ANXIETY AND STRESS

The methods and techniques described have helped many people to overcome their own anxiety problems. The approach is sensible and practical. The adrenaline rush, or fight-or-flight response, was needed for survival in hostile territory thousands of years ago. In today's world it causes the modern problems of Panic, Anxiety, Stress and Anger. The bad news is that it seems to be beyond our conscious control. We are told that it can only be moderated by medicines.

**However, there is good news**.

We can bring a counter-system, the recovery response, into operation by changing our language, body posture and breathing. We can play tricks that encourage our minds to adopt a peaceful state.

This book shows you how to use those natural resources that bring about the opposite reaction to panic, anxiety, stress and anger. We can easily promote feelings of relaxation, recovery and control.

## I KNOW WHAT IT'S LIKE!

Earlier in my life I suffered badly from panic attacks. I was unable to drive on motorways and so I planned routes that would avoid them. I am very aware that people shouting "pull yourself together" or "just get on with it" is ineffective. If I could have taken control, then I would have done so!

I no longer have problems with panic. I discovered the causes of my problems and I developed the ways to regain my life. Now, as a therapist with very many years of experience in helping people to control panic, anxiety, stress and anger, I want to share those methods. This book contains a successful approach to dealing with those problems. The methods and techniques have been carefully tried and tested with a great number of my clients. They work!

There are no lectures on what you should do; only help in using means to liberate yourself from that thing that seems to dominate your life, but seems to be beyond your control.

In this book the fillers have been eliminated and the verbiage cut. This book contains quality rather than quantity. I am sure that you want to find help without chapters of waffle to wade through. That is what I needed back in those bad days.

The information given in the breathing, posture and language sections of this book will help you as it has helped thousands of my clients in the past.

Read the chapters on breathing, posture and language over again. Take your time, do the exercises. You will be amazed at the difference those things make.

The exercises have to be done on a daily basis. They are set to ensure that you relax yourself before an event that used to worry you, and then they maintain you through any problems that arise. It is as if anxiety sits on a scale. Let us add representational numbers. Zero is being fast asleep and one hundred is at the worst possible level of panic. If stress and anxiety are at fifty and we go about our day at seventy, then it only takes thirty to take us way over the edge. However, if we start the day at twenty, then it takes a huge amount to get us anywhere near panic.

There are therefore two strategies.

The first is to do the breathing, posture and language exercises to bring our stress levels down. Just because they seem easy, it may seem to be a trivial waste of time to devote two minutes in the morning to laying on your back lifting a book into the air. The point is; you are lowering the base line.

An example will help. You have a pond that holds one hundred litres of water. Each morning the level is fifty or sixty. When it rains heavily, the pond overflows causing all sorts of damage. If your pond starts at twenty, it might fill up to fifty or sixty, but it never overflows. The breathing and posture exercises empty out the stress from your reservoir. The more you do it, the easier it becomes.

The second strategy is to watch the levels during the day and if they rise too far or too fast then you empty them as much as possible. With our pond example, during heavy rain, equivalent to something horrible happening to you on the train, in the car, in the supermarket or whatever, you take time out to empty some water to prevent an overflow. When the rain stops you continue to empty out the water, or in your case, the stress.

The only problem that exists with these stress busting techniques is in getting people to do them. If you went to your doctor and he gave you pills that made you able to cope you would take them as prescribed. All I am asking you to do is to devote four minutes per day, two in the morning and two in the evening, in order for you to feel the way you have wanted for, possibly, years and years.

Make a start now. Read the chapters on breathing, posture and language again. Practice the exercises and within a couple days, you WILL feel better.

# CHAPTER NINE

## PHOBIAS

### PUBLIC SPEAKING

A fear of public speaking is a major issue with people. All the signs of the fight or flight response are exhibited. The speaker's heart races, there may be copious sweating. There may be freezing. He/she wants to run away from the audience. The person rushes through the speech, panting for breath.

Is this familiar? Well, help is on the way.

Although the causes are usually from bad experiences, there is relief without going back to the times when the speaker was ridiculed in a school class, or when they felt bad at their wedding after a stag or hen night.

There are simple rules to follow:

1. If possible, make contact with your audience ahead of your talk. A loud "hello" suffices.

2. Remember that your audience is there to learn something from you rather than to be critical.

3. Practice your breathing rather than your speech. When there would be punctuation in written speech, take a SLOW in breath to your diaphragm and slide down the words on the other side. Breathe slowly and deeply every time you pause on a punctuation mark.

For example, *(Breathe in slowly)* "Good evening ladies and gentlemen. *(Breathe out. Breathe in slowly)* I would like to welcome you all to this talk. *(Breathe out. Breathe in slowly)* You may remember the last time we were all together. *(Breathe out. Breathe in slowly)* That was when my father..."

Practice those few lines to gain the idea of pace. It might seem laboured to you, but it is the best way to speak. Rushing gets you out of breath and makes you feel anxious.

4. You should speak as if describing a complicated matter to a stupid person!

5. Slow down your delivery. The faster you speak then the more you gasp for breath.

6. Use your hands. If something is big, make a big gesture. If something is high, point upwards. If you are welcoming people to a function, gather them in with your hands like an evangelical preacher.

7. Move around. This prevents you from freezing and gives your audience a dimension of movement.

8. If you worry about where to look, then slowly scan your audience from one side to the other without looking at anybody in particular. The audience is watching your head move and feels included.

OK, smarty pants, I can hear you say. How will eight simple points help me? Well. They will. Those little things have helped business folk, lawyers, fathers of brides, best men and many others. The best thing to do is go over them again and again and practice in your mind. When you make your mind believe you have given a great speech by mentally rehearsing, then when it comes to the actual event, your mind will take it in its stride.

The following are suggestions that help you to enjoy public speaking:

I breathe gently into my stomach when I speak.

I imagine I am speaking to my close family.

The audience is listening because they want to hear what I have to say.

The audience is friendly. They like me.

I speak slowly and draw pictures with my hands and body to illustrate what I am saying.

I copy live presenters on the TV to see how they do it.

Public speaking is fun.

**Now, using the positive language of hypnotherapy, write your own suggestions and check them against the 'words to avoid' list given earlier.**

# FLYING

It is a strange thing to say but for all the very many flying phobics that I have treated, I have yet to meet one who was actually scared of flying. Somewhat ironically, flying phobias seem to have little to do with flying.

Aircraft become symbols of fears and traumas, which need a place to rest. This might partly be the result of flying being perceived as an alien experience. We have all suffered the jealousies of not being able to fly like birds. Super-humans, 'Superman' for example, occupy childhood fantasies. Time teaches us that this fantasy world is never a reality.

More than three million people fly each day. It is the safest way to travel. Aircraft usually carry large numbers of passengers, so on the rare occasions when there is a crash, the story gets a lot of coverage which reaches the personal imaginations of lots of people. Car crashes get less coverage but are responsible for far more deaths. The airline, Virgin, makes the claim that flying is eighteen times safer than staying at home.

One common factor in flying phobias, as with others, is the fear of loss of control.

To get started on your flying phobia, think about all associations that you have with flying. Write them down and then start your own analysis. One common cause is a person's parent flying away on a business trip when the person was a child. It is difficult for a child to comprehend the need for an executive to fly to a meeting. Bags are packed and 'good-byes' are said. The child concludes that the aircraft is an evil thing that brings about separation.

Another cause is when arguments and misery have occurred on a holiday that involved flying. The aircraft acquires an emotionally negative value.

Based on case studies, I have listed some of the unconscious reasons why people develop a fear of flying, below. Compare these to your own list.

## 1. "if only".

This is unconsciously assigning blame to aircraft for bringing about a series of circumstances that were life changing. For example:

"If only father had not flown to xyz, then he would not have met 'Jane', and my parents would have been happily married, etc., etc."

"If only the honeymoon had been better."

"If only my husband had not travelled for his career."

"If only we had not moved (flown) abroad, then my husband might have drunk less, our son might not have been so threatened by my husband, etc., etc."

Flying, to the phobic, had become a means to a less than desirable end. So, rather than blaming the father or husband, the aircraft took the responsibility for disaster. It was the 'thing' that created the situation in unconscious terms. We have this innate need to assign blame to something or someone totally innocent of the outcome.

## 2. Similarity of object/experience.

Sometimes there has been an unconscious association between fear and an object that was almost incidental to an event.

Being trapped on a garage roof whilst an Air Show was taking place having climbed out of a window to watch the planes, is one example. Within this, intense feelings of being excluded from the family might have been created which indirectly happened after the phobic's first flight when it was discovered that the person's parents had split.

Fear can be transferred to 'a like' object such as an aircraft wing representing the metal roof where the person was stuck.

### 3. Culpability.

Sometimes there has been a fear of responsibility for potentially 'making bad things happen' to those people who are loved. Flying represents impending pleasure, so the phobic suffers guilt at the thought that he/she is endangering their loved ones on the same flight because he/she is thinking of their own enjoyment. The important thing to remember is that restricting a child's under-standing of the world is far more hurtful than enabling something wonderful to be experienced.

The culpability problem can also arise when children are left behind and the phobic worries about what would happen is he/she did not return.

### Control

The linking theme with the above is that of control. With "if only" the inability to control external events is considered to be responsible for 'blame'.

Likewise with "similarity of object/experience", if the person on the garage roof had been able to control the situation by getting down, the situation would have been more acceptable.

"Culpability" also shows the sufferer's inability to control a situation. Sometimes six-year-old girls assume that their father left home because they were not good enough rather than recognising the strife between husband and wife.

In my life I have been on aircraft in Force 9 gales, stacked above Nashville for two hours in a 360 degree thunderstorm, and so on. All I have discovered is that there is always time to help people who are worried about flying. I seem to attract them like a magnet. I have never been worried myself. I trust planes and the professional nature of pilots.

Anyway, it is not usually the case that flying phobias are created by bad flying experiences. Very often they appear to be the result of the projection of unfortunate experiences which are separate to flying, which then become attached to aircraft, or the outcome of flying. This is a result of the sense of ghoulish fascination with aircraft crashes by TV, newspapers and film-makers.

In order to treat such phobias it appears very necessary to find the original cause of the feelings of distress or panic, and subsequently change the negative feeling about flying to positive outcomes.

Hopefully, your list and mine will have triggered some of the negative associations that you have made and have enabled you to deal with them.

Now the process involves exposing the emotions which were a part of the underlying cause and thereby nullifying them.

**Making new associations**.

• Sit in a chair as you will on an aircraft from now on. Imagine that you are actually on an aircraft that is about to take to the skies. Use slow diaphragmatic breathing to relax yourself. Sit with your legs uncrossed and ankles apart. Place your arms to each side of your body. When you are feeling in control, take the next step.

• Imagine, when you see the nose of the plane before you board, that you can see a big smile just below the cockpit windows, the eyes. Make it into a friendly cartoon plane.

• Imagine when the plane starts to accelerate that you are sitting in a fast sports car.

• As the plane accelerates, remember it always goes twice as far down the runway as you think it should. Never worry because you think it should be airborne more quickly.

• When the plane lifts off the sensation in the stomach is like the childhood pleasure of going over a humpback bridge.

• If the plane seems to slow down after take-off, it is because air traffic control has given the instruction to level out at a certain height, perhaps make a turn and proceed until told to climb again. Phobics will take this as a stall. It is supposed to happen.

• Noises experienced will include the variation in engine power, the wheels and flaps being retracted. The flaps are pieces of the wing that move in and out to make the wing area bigger for flying at slower speeds and smaller when the speed increases. All this is supposed to happen.

• The most wonderful noise is when the aircraft is airborne and you hear the clanking of metal. This means that the cabin crew is releasing the food and drinks trolleys.

• When taking off, imagine the plane to be like a big swan. On the taxi ways it seems to waddle. On the runway it is when the swan is paddling hard to gain speed. After lift-off, the swan flaps its mighty wings and rises above the river. It is doing what nature designed it to do, fly. It is enjoying the freedom of being off the ground. Aircraft are designed and built to incredible standards to fly. That is what they like doing.

• Imagine the looks of pride from your travelling companions.

• Compare the worst turbulence you can remember on

an aircraft with a drive in you car. Even on the flattest road you will bounce in your car seat. You ignore those feelings but on a plane they seem to be exaggerated. Imagine you are sitting in your car and let those feelings diminish to the level where they can be disregarded. Imagine a drink in front of you. In any turbulence the glass might slide but it remains upright. I remember flying for four hours seated next to a flying phobic. I put my glass on my knee as we went through some turbulence. It never fell off once. Guess how long a glass would stay upright in a car, even on a motorway.

• Sit back and relax, perhaps watch a film, have some food. Think about what you will do at your destination. This projects your mind beyond the flight and landing.

• The landing is straightforward. The engine pitch changes, the plane seems to slow down. Then you hear the wheels lower with the rush of wind against them, and then, maybe the flaps being extended. The aircraft turns to make its approach and then you feel the bump as the wheels touch the runway.

• Imagine that you are writing a post-card to family and/or friends, or even me, from your destination, telling them how much you enjoyed the flight. In order to imagine doing this, you have to believe that you really did enjoy the flight. This confirms at an unconscious level that the flying was easy.

• See yourself at the destination in a happy and calm frame of mind. This is different to times before. If you worried about your children see them enjoying exploring new horizons. You have freed, rather than trapped, them.

• It is important that you visualise yourself enjoying the return journey. You should be laying on a beach happy with the outward journey and looking forward to the return flight.

IMPORTANT. If you skipped the breathing, posture and language section to read the above, please refer to that section now and re-read the above.

## SUGGESTIONS FOR FLYING PHOBICS

I used to worry about flying but now I feel calm, confident and in control in a plane.

The bumps that used to upset me now feel like my car on a country road.

This flight is helping me to be with my family in a relaxed and beneficial way.

This holiday will be like a second honeymoon.

It is wonderful to experience different cultures and foods.

My children will learn a lot from this experience.

**Now, using the positive language of hypnotherapy, write your own suggestions and check them against the 'words to avoid' list given earlier.**

# SPIDERS, SNAKES AND CREEPY-CRAWLIES.

These phobias fit into a category known as atavistic phobias. This is where we seem to be predisposed to learn to dislike certain things that were dangerous in our primeval days on earth. They include spiders, snakes, lizards, frogs, birds and water. The fears that our cave ancestors developed are still in the system.

Fifty thousand years ago, those things were more dangerous than they are now because we live in countries where most of the poisonous species of those animals have been eliminated or contained. Water that we swim in is enclosed in pools or is watched by lifeguards. Although there can be danger from all these things, nonetheless we are at less risk than our ancestors were.

The spiders found in Europe are those which kill and consume creatures that propose a higher risk to humans than lions or tigers. The spiders in our houses eat flies and mosquitoes. There is only one species of venomous snake in Europe. In America, poisonous snakes live in the wild rather than in conurbations.

## What causes these phobias?

The fear probably comes from our modern relatives! Take the scenario where as a young person you were probably fascinated by a spider emerging into your view. They are funny things to watch. They are unable to run in straight lines and they are fundamentally scared of us humans. We are much bigger than they are and we are able to kill them with a rolled up newspaper or a shoe. They want to run away from us but they panic and make jerky movements.

Imagine that an adult spider phobic entered the room when you were a child. They saw a spider near their precious infant and they were frightened. They then perceived the spider as a threat and they shouted or screamed. This frightened you and you then immediately displaced, or misdirected, that created fear onto the object of attention, the spider.

Hey presto! Another spider phobic was formed. It seems more logical to you that it would be appropriate to develop a fear of the adult but instead, as a child, you were naturally inclined to locate the fear onto the object of focus. If you had become mother, father, brother or sister phobic that would have caused major problems in the household. The irony is that the person who made you spider phobic was him/herself created in the same way.

The situation can be repeated with the sight of a snake in a newspaper, pet shop or on the television. When your parent shuddered, then the fear of the object transferred to you.

It can be duplicated by having a frog dropped down a shirt or blouse.

It is repeated by young fishermen throwing bait maggots into a person's face.

It happens when non-swimming parents watch their children in a pool and keep warning them of the dangers.

Fear is easily learnt, so the release from the phobia is straightforward as well.

**So, how do I get rid of my fears?**

Make friends with your enemies. Images that are held are so emotionally charged that it might seem difficult to contemplate making friends, yet is it easy.

## SPIDERS

Take five! Think of spiders as being terrified of you. Nobody explains their fears to you. All they want to do is stay alive. In the same way that you have an inherited fear of them, they have a greater fear of you. That is why they run. They want to seek safety so when you see a spider run across a room, it is searching for somewhere that is free of descending shoes and newspapers. They never attack. Even the poisonous spiders in Australia only defend themselves. Unfortunately, they sometimes overdo it, but in Europe there is no risk. All that spiders want to do is to catch flies that would otherwise land on your food. They want to consume mosquitoes that want to suck your blood.

Imagine the spider to be your guardian angel when on the ceiling and your best friend when on the ground. Imagine it in a cartoon sort of way with a big smile on its face every time it catches something that would otherwise hurt you.

Spiders are allies rather than enemies. Flies will put remnants of dog faeces on your meals and on the food your children will eat. They never care about health and safety. Flies carry illnesses. And they, like mosquitoes, seek out their food. However, spiders trap those pests for us and protect humans. They never walk in foul droppings and then climb onto our dinner. They make webs and, like fishermen, they catch those flying dangers for us.

My grandparents were farmers in the early twentieth century. They were unable to afford pesticides even if they had been available. They lived in an environment that was potentially dangerous. Cow dung, pig dung and chicken droppings were part of the scenery. Everything that flies love to land on. My grandparents milked the cows everyday, and flies love milk.

The only protection available was the spider. They never caught any infections from the spiders and had a wonderful expression that would have dated back hundreds of years. "If you want to live and thrive, let a spider stay alive." That is true, I promise you. Spiders are our protectors against disease. You may avoid picking them up and cuddling them, but because there is nothing to be afraid of, pick them up using a glass and a piece of cardboard and release them back into nature. You might be grateful one day! As an aside, have you ever met anybody who has been hurt by an average spider? The answer is no, I am sure.

**Now, using the positive language of hypnotherapy, write your own suggestions and check them against the 'words to avoid' list given earlier.**

### SNAKES

Fifty thousand years ago, snakes would have been a bigger threat than they are now. They would have been more numerous and medical aid would have been difficult to find. Adders are a protected species today. They have become fairly rare.

Snakes are either venomous or non venomous. In Europe, we have only one venomous snake and that is less of a threat than a cold or flu. Apparently, the last recorded fatality from an adder bite in the UK was over thirty years ago and that was a child.

Making friends with snakes is difficult because they are so difficult to find. With any snake, it is best to avoid attempts to catch or handle them. Most of the rare adder bites that have occurred followed when people have tried to catch them. They, like all creatures, will defend themselves when threatened. They have the fight or flight response as well and, most often, choose flight.

It is a good idea to reassure yourself that the risk that you will be bitten by a snake is tiny. Search on the Internet under Adder Bites, and you will see that their reputation is undeserved.

A good treatment is familiarisation. Visiting zoos and looking at snakes will wear down your fear. If you are able to handle a snake under the guidance of a keeper, so much the better. You will start to realize that snakes never seek out phobics. They just want to live in peace. They are never the vindictive creatures that have been created by Hollywood. Those are from the creation of fear for profit.

If you do see a snake in the wild, certainly your heart will beat faster. Avoid it and it will avoid you.

**Now, using the positive language of hypnotherapy, write your own suggestions and check them against the 'words to avoid' list given earlier.**

# CHAPTER TEN

## PERSONAL PROBLEMS

### ANGER MANAGEMENT

ANGER DESTROYS LIVES. It destroys relationships. Rather than learning how to live with your anger you must learn how to get rid of it.

Anger is an outcome of the fight or flight response. It is potentially the most dangerous inheritance from our primeval past. Back then we had to protect ourselves from predators, including other humans. We had to hunt for, and kill, our prey. We had to use adrenaline to run faster, punch harder and frighten away those creatures we were too weak to defend against.

In our more recent history, the war cry, the threatening gestures in battle and the intended intimidation of others was vital to staying alive. How inappropriate those things have become in a bar, in an office or at home!

Anger is often an expression of frustration that is misdirected at others. We might become angry with our boss and because we are worried that we could lose our jobs, we take that anger out on our families. This vents our frustrations but causes bigger problems that in their turn create more anger.

The process of displacement, or misdirection, is a difficult one to describe but an example serves better. A man who becomes angry with his wife might just be venting feelings that he developed as a child towards his mother but was too small to express them. When he grows into the position of having a partner who, for whatever reason, reminds him of his childhood, then that bottled up rage detonates and hurts the person he loves the most. This never justifies the anger but shows that it is often inappropriate and totally out of place. Nor does it suggest in any way that the man should become angry with his mother. As a mature person he needs to understand what happened in his childhood and come to terms with his life as it is in the present day. All he needs, like everybody else, is love and to be seen in a positive light. That never comes from expressing himself in an angry, violent or verbally abusive way.

We have to become used to living in a society that uses different laws to those of the fang and claw if we want to be happy.

Anger can be dealt with by tackling a great number of areas. If anger is a major outcome of your fight or flight response then:

## AVOID

### Alcohol
Avoid alcohol if this relates to your anger. Drinking to excess has become a part of modern life. It helps people to lose inhibitions, or in other words, lose control of social customs that have enabled us to live together in small social spaces. Fifty thousand years ago there was a lot of space. Now we are cramped together in towns, cities and on motorways. When people drink and lose control there is a temptation to express those frustrations on the nearest person physically or emotionally.

### Judging other people.
Avoid judging other people. Again, because we lack space, we form opinions about others and we assume that we know their value. We rarely do.

### Carrying grudges.
Avoid carrying grudges. We want to seek revenge for assumed wrongs. Back in time, if a bear killed our friends then we wanted to seek revenge by killing the

bear. That had a survival value. Carrying a grudge against other people never helps life to continue in today's society.

## Working out a response
Avoid working out a response to a comment before listening and understanding the other person's point of view.

## Assuming
Avoid assuming that you know what the other person is thinking. Unless we are psychic, we never know what the other person is thinking. We need to listen to find out. As once said "To assume makes an ASS out of U and ME."

## Jeopardising your future
Avoid jeopardising your future by being rash and out of control. A punch thrown at somebody WILL change your life for the worse. Calling your partner foul names will have a negative effect on your relationship that time is unable to heal.

## Lecturing to make a point.
Avoid lecturing to make a point. This is where you only want to talk rather than listen. When you lecture other people you look and sound like a fool rather than a professor.

## Being determined to change the other person's point of view to yours.
Avoid being determined to change the other person's point of view to yours. You are aggressively telling the other person why you are right and they are wrong. Are you always right? No! Sometimes you think you are, though! Listen to what the other person is saying and if you disagree, then 'beg to differ'.

## Being self-absorbed.
Avoid being self-absorbed. You are likely to behave like

a small child having a tantrum because you are not getting your way. Act like an adult as an alternative.

**INSTEAD**

### Listen
Listen to the content of the conversation rather than the noise. Understand and comprehend what is being said.

### Consider
Consider the longer-term implications of angry outbursts. Divorce, jail or job loss?

### Learn to release feeling safely.
Vent your anger by throwing slices of bread to (never at) the ducks. They will feed and you will feel better.

### Accept
Accept that others' views are different to yours sometimes. We all have different backgrounds and cultures.

### Work
Work to achieve 'win/win' solutions rather than total victory. Very often we want to win arguments at all costs. That is a win/lose situation where you win the argument and the other person loses. A win/win situation is where both parties feel that they have given a little in order to gain.

### Live in the present
Live for today rather than the past. Being angry at past outcomes will never bring about future peace. Remember the example at the beginning of this chapter.
### Look at the situation with empathy.
Understand the other person's point of view even if you disagree with it.

## Recognise physical signs of anger
Recognise physical signs of anger such as muscle tension in the neck and stomach. Remember these are signs of stress and anger is part of the same reaction, the **fight** or flight response. Unclench your fists. Slow your breathing. Get a control of your body.

## Be able to take 'time-out'.
Agree to walk away, (flight), rather than allow an intensity of anger to grow, (fight). Agree with the other person that if you feel angry then you will state your need for a 'time out' and that you will walk away for, say, five or ten minutes so that you will get thoughts in order rather than scream or shout or hit.

## Ask yourself if your angry outburst will cause happiness or misery.
We all want to be happy. If you say something when you are out of control, you will find misery rather than comfort. So ask yourself if an angry outburst will cause happiness or misery and act and speak to get happiness. We would all like to cuddle up to our partner this evening rather than be on the settee or, perhaps, be in jail.

## Remember the damage
Remember the damage that your anger caused in the past, and think of the happy future that will be built when you have learnt to control your outbursts.

## Remember that you have controlled
Remember that you **have** controlled your anger in a wide variety of situations before and then apply those controls to the present situation.

## Be concerned
Be concerned with giving and sharing rather than getting your own way. If your anger came from past events, then get your pleasure and happiness today by being in control and getting rid of your rages.

Anger is a dangerous problem because it involves other people and can include violence. This is a very short first-aid section. If you need help then there are anger management specialists who will help you.

Check with your doctor for names.

## SUGGESTIONS FOR ANGER

I used to be an angry person, but now I control my feelings of rage.

I am able to see the destructive side of my bad temper and I calm down.

I used to hurt people to show how tough I am, but I am able to control myself and that shows other people that I am strong within myself.

I am calm, confident and in control, now.

I now prefer happiness to anger.

**Now, using the positive language of hypnotherapy, write your own suggestions and check them against the 'words to avoid' list given earlier.**

## FERTILITY

Note. Although anxiety plays a role in preventing conception, the following is unlikely to help in cases of defined biological problems. However, it appears that IVF treatments are more successful in a relaxed frame of mind rather than in a stressed situation.

If we look back to our primeval selves, it made sense to breed when times were good and to avoid becoming pregnant when times were unsafe. If food was likely to become scarce through crop failure, bad weather or the migration of our prey then we became at risk from starvation and our subsequent predation by the large animals on the plains.

It seems that a woman could, and can, be prevented from becoming pregnant by using the unconscious resources of her body and mind. If, during the bad times, she conceived then the embryo, and then the baby would be at risk. She would be at risk herself. If she died then she would eliminate all chances of breeding in the future. Nature is cruel and it is kind. It stands to reason, intuitively rather than scientifically, that becoming pregnant or remaining childless is related to the emotional and security circumstances of the prospective parents.

This also, perhaps, contributes to a lower sperm count for stressed men.

### CAUSES OF ANXIETY IN FERTILITY PROBLEMS

1. Employment and income doubts. If a couple relies on two salaries to pay the mortgage, provide food, buy holidays and so on, then the prospect of a baby arriving could upset the lifestyle and more to the point, the security of the parents. Is having a baby what you want or, do you want a more self-centred lifestyle? Nobody can afford a baby, but somehow all parents do.

2. Marital problems. If either partner doubts that the relationship will be sustained into the future, then the same issues of security of life will be to the forefront. This is an issue that can only be resolved by open discussion and is beyond the scope of this book. Find a counsellor if necessary.

3. Pressure to conceive. Some people feel pressured when attempting to conceive. Maybe one partner wants a baby and the other doubts. Perhaps the parents of the couple attempting conception want grandchildren. Conception requires a male and a female input. If both potential parents want to have a baby it is their decision and nobody else's. If your decision upsets your mother-in-law, it is her problem rather than yours.

4. In a similar way, having children is not a competitive sport. Keeping up with, or overtaking siblings is a no-no. Do what you want and do it when you want to. Be yourselves, strive to reach your own goals.

**Getting rid of anxiety**

1. Learn to relax. Follow the language, breathing and posture exercises detailed in this book. Remember, one of the results of anxiety is freezing, maintaining the status quo. If that means remaining childless, relax and let your body decide what change will take place in your lives. Tell your body that you are in a good situation and you are ready to have a child.

2. Stop having planned sex! Having sex to make a baby is counter-productive. It creates anxiety rather than a child. It takes away the pleasure, and pleasure is one of the greatest things that helps you to relax.

3. Start making love. So many wannabe mothers who have had initial problems conceiving follow the route of planning their love lives like a military campaign. They keep ovulation charts, obsess about their temperatures, follow diets from women's magazines and as a result

become anxious. Start making love in the way you did in earlier years when you worried about becoming pregnant rather than worrying, as you do now, about being unable to conceive. Stop planning your sex life and start enjoying love making for the pleasure it gives. After all, the reason that sex is fun is to encourage us to procreate. It is the incentive that we need. Making love for fun rather than having sex for conception will remove a lot of the natural inhibitors of becoming pregnant.

4. Go for the orgasm. This is as natural as it should be. There are biological reasons why a female orgasm contributes to the movement of sperm to where it should be. Even if you orgasm later than your male partner, there are ways in which a woman can still achieve an orgasm after him. Get him to do some work! Enjoy!

5. As yucky as this sounds, lay in bed after making love. Douching away the sperm quickly is never going to help.

6. Relax before you make love. Have a bath. Get your man to give you a massage. Make making love a pleasure rather than a process. You are a human-being rather than a heifer waiting for the farmer's bull. You are a woman waiting for romance.

7. Love making is a relaxation if there is no pressure to perform. Men get problems when under pressure to perform in love making. That applies to women as well. Their performance is self-evaluated in terms of whether or not she can make a baby. Enjoy your love life and let a baby be the result. That is the more natural way, the way of our cave dwelling ancestors.

8. Place yourself in the mental state where you think of the baby as a child. This places your mind beyond the conception and pregnancy. You mind anticipates an outcome. This relieves the worries that you might have about miscarriage.

**Words to make you think**.

Remember the stories of the women who became pregnant after adopting a child. Why? They relaxed.

Remember the girls who got pregnant from having a one night stand. Why? They were having fun, they were relaxed. The last thing they wanted was a baby.

Stop <u>trying</u> to have a baby, have one.

## SUGGESTIONS FOR FERTILITY

I conceive of the time when I am pregnant. (This might sound corny but it is packed with positivity.)

I had problems conceiving <u>but now</u> I realise it is a natural result of enjoyable love making.

I thought that getting pregnant was difficult, <u>but now</u> I know that is much easier than I thought.

All my ancestors, since life started, had babies.

**Now, using the positive language of hypnotherapy, write your own suggestions and check them against the 'words to avoid' list given earlier.**

**IBS**

**PLEASE NOTE.**
**Before reading on, please ensure that you have consulted your doctor about any problems concerning your problems. Although stress and anxiety can cause or aggravate IBS, there are more serious causes that need to be investigated.**

Back in time, if you and a chum were being chased by a lion or another predator then the one to be caught and eaten would have been the slowest. As any follower of horse racing will tell you, the way to slow a runner down is to handicap it by adding weight. The winner of our primeval race would be the lightest, all other things being equal. A part of the fight or flight response is to make us empty our bowels, bladder and/or our stomachs in order to lose weight. Nervous and anxious people are known to wet themselves when under threat. Filling our pants is another problem for frightened people. There is a hierarchy of parts to empty. First the bladder. It contains liquid that is unusable. Next the bowels. Although the solid waste is simply waste, it does contain water that is reabsorbed into the blood stream. The last is the stomach. It contains partly digested food that still has a nutritional value.

It should come as no surprise that what has been described as irritable bowel syndrome is related to stress and anxiety. It should also come as a relief that relaxation is known to help to alleviate the symptoms. When we are anxious our body naturally diverts blood from the skin and gut to the muscles where it is needed for fighting or running. It makes little difference to you if you are about to be eaten by a lion. The problem arises when we are perpetually stressed, perhaps from having IBS. We restrict the blood flow to the gut and we end up with digestive troubles.

Doing the breathing, posture and language exercises on a regular basis will help to take away the stress and some, perhaps all, of the discomfort. The language to be used in your thinking should take the form of: "I used to worry about going out to xxx, but now I am calm, confident and in control." Allow yourself to relax and allow yourself to be in control. When the unconscious threat that was perceived has gone, you will find that your gut returns to a more natural state.

**Make time to relax in your daily routine**.

Remember that stress slows down digestion and this causes sluggishness in the system. The gut is a tube that runs from the mouth to the anus and it needs a supply of blood and digestive juices in order to work on your food to extract the nutritional content. A good supply of blood is also needed to absorb and transport the nutritional substances to the parts of the body where they are needed. Relaxation allows blood to return to your gut to enable digestion to take place more efficiently. When that happens then your IBS is alleviated and then it is controlled.

**Words and idioms to make you think.**

We have some strange and interesting idioms that point to the connection between IBS and anxiety. Please excuse the words if they offend you:

Bit off more than you can chew.
Bore your arse off.
Butterflies in the stomach.
Eyes bigger than belly.
He is full of shit.
I am busting a gut.
I do not have the stomach for that.
I feel sick to the stomach.
I find that he is a pain in the arse.
I hate his guts.
I have a gut feeling that something is wrong.
On an empty stomach.

Scare the shit out of me.
Spill your guts.
Strong stomach.
Tight arse.
Work my guts out.

And so on and on.

Perhaps more positive idioms are:

I've got a good feeling inside.
Let me digest the information about IBS
I'll chew it over.


**RULE NUMBER ONE**
**LEARN TO RELAX ON A REGULAR BASIS.**

**Now, using the positive language of hypnotherapy, write your own suggestions and check them against the 'words to avoid' list given earlier.**

## INSOMNIA

There is an old joke that says that the best cure for insomnia is a good night's sleep. Ha, ha! However, there is truth in that. Once you get into the routine of sleeping well then the miracle happens. You continue to sleep well.

## So how do I start getting a good night's sleep, or how do I stop getting a bad night's sleep?

The following will sound a little ridiculous, but it works to cause insomnia. Every night when an insomniac goes to bed they think:

a) "I will get another night when I will go to sleep and then wake up at 3.00 am. I will toss and turn and not get back to sleep.

b) I will get into bed and lay awake and I will not get to sleep again.

c) I will fall in and out of sleep as usual.

Let us break the cycle. Every time an insomniac thinks those thoughts then he/she is giving their mind negative suggestions that will be followed.

Stories abound about sound sleepers who never set an alarm clock but always wake up when they want. They tell their minds what to do. Then suggestions are used positively.

**Step one**. Make friends with your bed. Over time it has become a hostile place. It has become something to be dreaded. This is the bit that sounds silly! Go into your bedroom and talk out loud to your bed. It is your friend, really. It is the place where you used to sleep well. Perhaps it the place where you have made love. Perhaps it is the place where your children were conceived. Maybe your children jump, or used to jump onto the bed on a Sunday morning. Remember the good times; change your negative thoughts about your bed into happy ones. Love your bed, stop feeling bad about it.

**Step two.** Change your thinking. Say to yourself, "I used to have problems getting to sleep, staying asleep, sleeping on and off (or whatever the problem was), but NOW I fall asleep quickly and sleep soundly until whatever time I want to wake up." Sounds simple, doesn't it. Hey! Who said good has to be difficult? People you know who sleep well never think that they will have a problem. So follow suit. Assume that your problem was in the past and that from now on you sleep as well as them.

When you are sleeping well you will actually see the funny side of the joke.

Suggestions for sleeping well:

I love my bed. It is where I feel safe and secure.

I go to sleep easily, now, and I sleep wonderfully until? o'clock. (This is the time you want to awaken.)

When I was a child I used to sleep well. Now those wonderful nights have returned. I now sleep as I did when I was a young person.

My children were conceived, born and raised in a bed. Beds are friendly and safe places and I can trust them. They looked after the security of my children when they were vulnerable.

**Now, using the positive language of hypnotherapy, write your own suggestions and check them against the 'words to avoid' list given earlier.**

## CONFIDENCE

I am not really sure if I can help you with this one.

Now having set the scene, I will continue to show you how you can gain all the confidence that you need. This is all about persuading your mind that you are as able as anybody and you can do anything that you desire.

Think of the most confident and successful person you can. You are so genetically close to that person as a human being that anything they can do so can you. (Allowing for physical limitations, of course. An eighty year old is unlikely to win a gold medal in a 100 metre race in the Olympics, but that is another issue. We are here to get you to achieve your goals.)

The first part of building confidence is to establish your goals in a bold way. Avoid your negative inner dialogue that might say, "I want to ask for a pay rise but my boss will probably think I am being greedy and will fire me."

So when you do ask you will say something like, "I want a pay rise, please. I hope you do not think I am being greedy. It's just that Mary got one the other day and I think it's unfair." This is conveyed with a look of submissiveness and the voice trails away. So, is it a surprise when the boss turns you down? You have demonstrated that you are weak and that you will take "No" for an answer.

For a few moments, put yourself in Mary's shoes. How did she ask? She walked in with her head high and a smile on her face. Her request was made in a different way. She stated that she needed some more money as she was working hard and helping the company to run smoothly and profitably. This stated that she was contributing to the welfare of the company. She implied that the company would be worse off without her and that as she had asked for more then if she received a negative reply then she might look for another employer who would appreciate her hard work more. So, this could be seen as a veiled threat, but it proves that Mary is strong.

When you step out of Mary's shoes, take part of her with you. The intention is that you become more confident rather than aggressive. You have as much value as she does but she has a different approach to life. She knows what she wants and how to get it. You know what you want but you are preoccupied with failure in obtaining your goals. Seek out what you want and practice getting it in your mind. Act out role-playing in your mind. Rehearse being Mary or any other example you can think of in your personal or business life. Add celebrities, successful famous business people. Step into their psyches, their mind sets, and imagine how they feel when being confident. Think about their posture, body language, tone of voice and the looks they give and so on. Analyse them and copy them. It makes a difference that is very powerful.

Work on your language exercises. Stop trying to get a pay rise with all its implied failure, go and get yourself one. This applies to all areas of your life. When you want something, want it enough to get it. This might mean changes in your life. You might have to change your clothes. Look at the appearance of successful people you know, or those you see in the newspapers and on TV. They are thriving because they are acting out winning roles. Carl Jung, the great psychologist, talked about the 'masks' we wear. They are the costumes we wear when we are acting, and actors take on the qualities of the people in the roles they are playing. In real life they are different. Method actors study the types of people they portray and take on their characteristics. They watch and copy. When they do that they become the other person along with their traits.

As you want to win, take on the characteristics of winners. They are different to losers. Look at Richard Branson. He is relaxed and casual in appearance but he has a record of success that is rarely equalled. He suits his role and he wins because he seems like a winner. He creates confidence in the people around him because he has confidence in abundance.

Make affirmations for yourself. Tell yourself everyday that you are a winner. Tell yourself what you want and how what you want is with you now. Winners are winners rather than becoming winners in the future. Be a winner now and act it out.

"I am a best selling author, now." Hey, you bought my book, didn't you? Let it happen to you by telling yourself that what you want is what you are.

**Do this exercise, now.**

Think of a goal that has eluded you because you have lacked confidence. Write it down. Now think of somebody who seems to have an abundance of confidence. Pretend to be that person and watch how he/she achieves your goal. What did they do? How did they act? How did they dress and speak. How did they hold their head and their gaze? What was the secret?

Now write down the difference between them and you. **NOW,** become that person. Now you have the strategy to make the changes you need.

Also see the chapter on **Goal Achievement and Visualisation**

**Now, using the positive language of hypnotherapy, write your own suggestions and check them against the 'words to avoid' list given earlier.**

## SEXUAL PROBLEMS.

One of the major causes of impotence in men is smoking. If you are a smoker and you are reading this part, then it is time to stop. The pleasure derived from an intimate relationship far outweighs the perceived pleasures of smoking. See the section on stopping smoking in this book.

Another cause is an excess of alcohol. Heavy and long term drinking will steal more pleasures than sex from you. The treatment of drinking problems is beyond the scope of this book. If alcohol is an issue for you, then seek help.

We have talked about the fight or flight response. That is the red alert state and causes the problems. The opposing branch is the one we are using to bring about the alleviation of the problems. The names of those two branches are long and unwieldy. The fight or flight response is call the sympathetic branch of the autonomic nervous system. The opposing system, the relaxation response, is called the parasympathetic branch.

Medical students learn the names in a straightforward way, Point and Shoot. P and S. To get an erection, a man needs to experience the parasympathetic branch, in other words he needs to be relaxed. When he ejaculates the sympathetic branch kicks in, in other words he becomes excited.

Putting this into our primeval world, when a man felt safe and away from danger he could get an erection so he could enjoy himself and possibly breed. It also made sense that if danger suddenly loomed, he would ejaculate into the woman and get the heck out of there. Manners were invented later, perhaps!

There are very few physical dangers in the modern

bedroom but there are enemies within the psyche. Fear of failure can bring about failure. The man feels pressurised to pleasure his mate and this anxiety makes him orgasm too soon because he feels threatened. On the other hand, the pressure for him to achieve an erection can stop it from happening. He needs to be relaxed. Then he can make love in a way that maintains the feeling of relaxation until the point comes when he wants to change his state so that he can ejaculate. Life can be complicated.

We are surrounded by sexual images in films and on the television progressing from loves scenes to pornography. Never do we see the hero fail to satisfy the heroine. Standards are set against which men are expected to perform. Let us get real! They are fiction.

**Impotence**

Let yourself relax, stop getting excited about having sex. Put your mind into an easy condition by changing your breathing and by letting your muscles ease into a tension free state. If your partner is sympathetic then ask her to take pressure away by accepting that this might be an erection free night.

Sex therapists have used this method for many years. Allow the clients to touch each other under the instruction, "Do not make love." A wonderful use of the negative suggestion. If it happens, use it, if it stays soft, nothing has been lost.

If your problem persists and as the causes of erectile dysfunction are many, it is better that I refer you to seek help from your doctor.

**Premature or Delayed Ejaculation**

Most of the above applies here as well. Worrying about ejaculating can make it happen, so you maintain relaxation throughout lovemaking. There are some other tricks that you can play. Try to 'come' as quickly as possible. Note the use of the word 'try', implying to your mind that it is a difficult thing to do. This is mirrored when people have problems ejaculating. They have developed a mind-set that prevents it from happening. They want it but have the thought that it is difficult and that it will not happen. This is an issue of self-fulfilling prophesies. The guy who wants to delay thinks that it will happen quickly and the guy who wants it to take place believes that it will never happen.

**ONLY READ THIS IF YOU WANT TO HAVE CONTROL OVER YOUR ORGASM.**

You will find that the problem you had will reverse. The premature ejaculator will have to wait for at least twenty minutes for it to happen no matter what you consciously decide. If you are failing to ejaculate then it will happen after twenty minutes no matter what you consciously decide. This is the state you have put yourself in. I am sorry, but I warned you about reading this.

**Now, using the positive language of hypnotherapy, write your own suggestions and check them against the 'words to avoid' list given earlier.**

**You might find it hard but it will come sooner or later. (Rather than jokes, those words are hints to point you in the right direction.)**

# JEALOUSY

This is a difficult area to cover because the causes are fairly diverse and I need to avoid making matters worse.

Some people are jealous because they lack self esteem and believe that their partner will want somebody else. Refer to the sections on confidence above and goal setting below.

However it might be that you have a history of bad experiences that have given you the idea that men/women are untrustworthy. This needs the help of a therapist to eliminate your doubts about your partner's views of you.

Another cause is where the jealous person has had affairs, or is having them, and projects their behaviour onto their partner. In the short term, stop. Then seek help as mentioned above. There is probably a reason why you feel the need to have affairs or to have the positive attention from other people than your partner.

These notes are given because, once again, it is a tricky problem to treat via a book and it is important that negative ideas are avoided by the reader.

Personal help is needed to get to the bottom of this problem but, in the short-term, seek out which category you might fit into. Talk to your partner about your concerns. Sometimes the solution is staring you in the face.

# CHAPTER ELEVEN

## HABITS AND ADDICTIONS

### STOP SMOKING

ACCORDING TO A STUDY that was conducted a few years ago, hypnosis is the most effective way to stop smoking. Breathing techniques are the second most effective way.

I am a clinical hypnotherapist with many years of experience of helping people to rid themselves of unwanted problems and habits. That expertise is brought to you to help you to stop smoking and to start living.

The two things that people want to avoid when they stop smoking are putting on excess weight and withdrawal symptoms, so that is where we will start.

Smoking is very much a hand-mouth activity that reminds smokers of the comfort they felt whilst being suckled at their mothers' breasts. It seems to be no mere coincidence that many filter tips are actually nipple shaped and coloured. I'll pause a while whilst that horrible thought sinks in.

Why do cigarette companies go to the trouble of printing the paper that goes into the mouth?

Anyway, substitutions tend to be hand-mouth. Things such as fiddling with the hair, nail-biting and stuffing the mouth with food.

I will suggest a substitution to you very directly.

That is a sense of satisfaction in being a non-smoker. After all, you will look better because smoking takes blood from the skin, leaving it less well nourished than it should be. It is easy to spot an older smoker by the state of their skin.

You will also feel better. I understand that there are 4200 different chemicals in cigarette smoke, over 2000 of which are toxic, including cyanide, arsenic, acetone, formaldehyde and carbon monoxide to name just five out of more than 2000!

And you are going to smell better. As a smoker you may fail to notice how bad the smell of smoke on clothes, your hair and breath is. You will after you stop. And if you are male, as mentioned above, smoking is a major cause of impotence.

In short, you will feel the benefits of stopping, a great sense of satisfaction in having beaten that habit that holds so many in its grip.

There is one more thing that you will substitute, and that is contained within the next part that covers withdrawal symptoms.

Because I have no desire to be sued I have to be very careful about how I put this next part! I want you to consider the information that is professionally and carefully given about the addictiveness of nicotine.

It includes the claim that "nicotine is ten times more addictive than heroin." Well, I have treated many cigarette smokers and quite a few heroin addicts. It is far easier to get people to stop smoking than to get them off heroin.

In short, I believe that there is a mythology about nicotine that makes it seem more difficult to stop smoking than it actually is. I get lots and lots of recommendations from people who have stopped smoking using my methods. Those people recommend me because they were free of withdrawal symptoms. I have no magic but what I will do is explain what you thought withdrawal symptoms are.

**Do this exercise.**

Take a deep breath in and hold it for a few moments. Notice how your neck and shoulder muscles tightened. Notice how you pulled your stomach in.

As a culture, we have become high-chest breathers. We sit up straight, we puff up our chests. This is to the detriment of using the lower parts of our lungs.

The process of gas exchange in the lungs is independent of the breathing cycle. The lungs are excretory organs, which is why our breath smells of garlic the day after we eat it. Stale gases collect in the lower parts of our lungs. They increase in concentration until they start going back into the bloodstream. This makes us feel twitchy, irritable and bad.

Now, if you are right handed, put your left hand on your stomach and your right hand on your high chest. If you are left-handed do it the other way around.

Now take a deep breath in whilst trying to keep the hand on your chest still, and pushing the hand on your stomach out with the breath.

Difficult, isn't it!

Do it again.

Now put the hand that was on your chest up to your mouth. Go through the action of taking a long, deep puff on a cigarette. Did you notice that the hand on your stomach came out?

The ironic thing about smoking is that the only time a smoker seems to breathe correctly is when they are smoking. This is the key.

Take the example of a 20 a day smoker. He is a high chest breather but 20 times a day he smokes and in the process, flushes out the stale, waste gases in the lower parts of his lungs. When he tries to stop by will power, the waste gasses build up in his lungs, increase in concentration and re-enter the bloodstream. Those feelings of twitchiness, irritability and so on seem to be those feelings that have been described as withdrawal symptoms. I feel that they are mostly the natural physiological effects of the build up of waste products in the lungs going back into your system.

This explains why breathing techniques are so effective. Instead of using a cigarette as a stimulus to breathe correctly, all you have to do is use a breathing technique to breathe correctly. Simple, isn't it. And it works.

Follow the breathing exercises in this book and you will surprise yourself at how effective they are. The one below is specifically for people stopping smoking.

Take a deep breath into your stomach, ignoring your upper chest. Keep that part still. Strangely, it might help you to pretend that you are taking a deep puff on a cigarette. Hold that breath for a slow count of four, breathe out whilst saying the words 'I AM A NON-SMOKER' in your mind to yourself.

Do that twice more ensuring that you take your time.

If you feel slightly light-headed, that means that you have done it correctly! Isn't that the feeling you had when you smoked the first cigarette of the day? Now you know why. It was because you were breathing correctly.

Now you can do it without taking the harmful chemicals,

including tar, into your lungs. Think how much money you spent on something that helped you to breathe in the past. Now you can breathe safely and beneficially without inhaling those harmful products.

This is why you should build breathing techniques into your life to reduce your stress. Breathe deeply with every breath using this technique as a direct substitute for smoking.

It works. Ask the huge number of people I have seen over the past decade who have stopped smoking, free of what were thought to be withdrawal symptoms.

## THE "I AM A NON-SMOKER" TECHNIQUE:

1.  Sit in a chair in a safe place.

2.  Unfold your arms and place to the side.

3.  Uncross your legs, open them and place your heels on the ground

4.  Become aware of your breathing. If rapid, slow it down consciously.

5.  Relax your neck and shoulder muscles.

6.  Allow your stomach muscles to relax.

7.  Take a deep breath into the lower part of your lungs, allowing your stomach to expand. Remember that the upper chest will fill automatically so avoid filling your upper lungs.

Hold this breath for a slow count of 4. As you slowly expel the air from your lungs, say to yourself, in your mind, the words: "**I AM A NON-SMOKER**", and allow your whole body to relax, drooping your shoulders again as you do so.

8. Repeat this three more times, again saying the words, "**I AM A NON-SMOKER**" as you exhale.

When you have taken those 4 deep breaths, just allow the word "**I AM A NON-SMOKER**" to drift around in your mind and allow your shoulders, neck and stomach muscles to really ease out and soften.

# CHAPTER TWELVE

## STOP SMOKING SCRIPT

**The following script can be recorded and played back to enable you to experience the hypnotherapy sessions.**

**Alternatively, without wishing to read like a commercial, you can buy recordings of the sessions, spoken by the author, from http://www.emp3books.com**

THE FOLLOWING IS A HYPNOSIS SCRIPT that works to help people to stop smoking. If you are recording it, read the words as if you were telling a story. There is a belief that hypnosis is induced by speaking with a lacklustre monotone voice! No. Sound as if you were relaxing somebody rather than boring them to sleep. Record the words to a soft background of instrumental music if you can. Check copyrights though.

### Script

Ensure that you are in a safe and comfortable place, settle down and start to relax. Let yourself relax completely, and then, when you are ready, just take an extra deep breath into your stomach, and when you breathe out, let your eyes close and settle yourself down into a really comfortable position. All you need to do now is relax and listen to the sound of my voice.

You will be amazed at how easily you now stop smoking.
You will be surprised at the ease with which you now stop smoking.
You will take so much pride and pleasure at stopping smoking.
You will so happy at how easily you now stop smoking.
Now just let all outside thoughts fade away. Just relax

and let go. Just listen to the sound of my voice and let yourself settle down completely. It might surprise you, but during this you will be aware of other outside sounds, but just hearing these outside sounds will actually help you to relax even more.

So let yourself become still and quiet and for now nobody wants anything from you. You are in a safe and a peaceful place where you can just let go and enjoy being yourself. Your time is completely your own. All you have to do is relax. Breathe normally and listen to the sound of my voice.

I want you know to take a deep breath in and to hold it while you slowly count to four in your own mind to yourself. Now as you breathe out say to yourself the word 'relax' slowly in your own mind and as you say that word 'relax' just let yourself go. Just let all of your muscles sag and become limp.

Good.

I want you know to take another deep breath in and to hold it while you slowly count to four in your own mind to yourself. Now as you breathe out say to yourself the word 'relax' slowly and as you say 'relax' just let yourself go. Just let all of your muscles sag and become limp. Feel like a soft rag doll. Good.

Now let yourself become still and quiet and for now nobody wants anything from you. You are in a safe and peaceful place where you can just let go and enjoy being yourself. Your time is completely your own. Just relax and breathe normally, and listen to the sound of my voice.

I will now say the word 'RELAX' four times, and the fourth time I say that word 'RELAX', I want you then to let all your muscles relax completely, just as though you were drifting into a deep, a very deep and relaxing sleep. So stay in that comfortable position and just listen to the sound of my voice. Just listen while I say that word 'RELAX' four times, and the fourth time I say that word 'RELAX', I want you then to just let all your muscles sag, just let go completely, as though you were drifting into a very deep and relaxing sleep.

(1) 'RELAX'.
So just let your muscles start to relax and feel yourself getting more and more settled.
(2) 'RELAX'.
Settle down even more, relax even more....just let your muscles sag gently.
(3) 'RELAX'. Still settle more comfortably. Let your muscles sag even more. Feel like a soft rag doll.
(4) 'RELAX'.
Now just keep on relaxing every part of your body and your mind and imagine that you were just drifting off into a deep, a very deep and relaxing sleep.

Now as you are relaxing there, imagine yourself lying on a towel on a sandy beach on a warm sunny day. Just imagine that; just imagine yourself lying on a towel on a sandy beach on a warm sunny day.

Imagine you can see the waves out on the blue sea.

And you can hear the waves gently lapping on the shore.

You can smell the salt in the sea air.

You can feel the warmth of the sun as it shines up in the blue sky.

You're just relaxing, just enjoying these peaceful feelings of being calm, of feeling lazy and lethargic.
And you can see little yachts sailing out on the water.

And you can hear the sounds of birds singing in the

distance.

You can smell the scent of wild flowers being wafted in on the breeze.

You can feel the sand, soft and warm beneath your fingers.

And you're just lying there enjoying the moment and allowing yourself to relax.

You're enjoying just being on the beach in the warm sun. In that place where nobody needs anything from you. You are in a safe and a peaceful place where you can just let go and enjoy being yourself, where your time is completely your own. All you have to do is relax.

As you are lying there just think of the top of your head and let your scalp relax. Let the muscles on the top of your head ease out and soften.

From now on, every time you breathe in just imagine that you can feel relaxation flowing into the part of your body that you are thinking about. And every time you breathe out you will feel all tension being taken away with your breath and blown right away from you.

So just lie there and feel relaxation flowing in, and tension flowing out, every time you breathe in...and then out.

Now let the tiny muscles around your eyes relax. Let them soften. Feel them become peaceful.

And now let your forehead relax. Let any frown lines you find there just even out and disappear.
And the sun feels even warmer, even more comfortable as you breathe in calmness, and blow away tension.

And if you want, you can let your jaw relax and drop

open a little. And if you find saliva collecting in your mouth just gently swallow it and let it soothe and calm your throat.

Feel yourself drifting into a calm and peaceful sort of feeling.

Now relax those big muscles in your neck and shoulders. Let them go limp, feel them just go limp. Feel the peacefulness spreading through your neck and shoulders.

Your arms are becoming so relaxed now, all tensions are fading away.

This feeling of peacefulness is moving down your arms to your elbows. It's a calm and peaceful sort of feeling.

Now it is easing into your forearms, down into your wrists and down into your hands. You might even feel your fingers tingling with calmness as relaxation comes into them with each breath inwards and as tension disappears with every breath outwards.

Now relax your back, those big muscles either side of your spine just soften and sag as you continue to relax.

And let this feeling flow downwards to your buttocks and let any tension just ease away. Imagine yourself drifting into a calm and peaceful sort of feeling. A very relaxed and peaceful sort of feeling.

Now let any tension in your chest turn to a peaceful relaxation. Just let go and let your chest relax. Breathe in relaxation and calmness and let go of any tension you find as you exhale.

Now take a very deep breath and feel the air flow into your lungs.

Know that as a non-smoker your lungs will become cleaner and cleaner.

Now feel the calmness in your stomach. Feel your stomach gently rise and fall as you breathe.

Let it rise.
Let it fall.

Just relax as you allow yourself to drift deeper and deeper down into this very pleasant feeling as you drift deeper and deeper down into this nice, calm and pleasant feeling of hypnosis...now.

As you allow yourself to drift deeper and deeper down into this very pleasant state of relaxation.

And now feel that peacefulness in your pelvis. All the muscles there become calm and peaceful.

Let this feeling of relaxation flow slowly down to your thighs. Let those muscles just soften and become limp.

This feeling continues down into your calves and all of the tension that was there before has now dissolved away.

Now feel the calmness in your ankles.

And now in your feet.

And you may notice your feet are feeling light...
You may notice they're feeling heavy...

You may notice that you seem to have lost contact with them, altogether.

Whichever suits you the best.

Now feel the relaxation in your toes as you take that

inward breath and feel it enter your toes. This feeling just flushes away any remaining tension into your outward breath which you then just breathe away.

Feel relaxation in your whole body and your mind as you continue to lie on that beach in the sun allowing yourself to drift deeper and deeper still into this very pleasant feeling of complete relaxation.

**(The suggestions)**

• And as you're lying there you are thinking to yourself how amazed you are at how easily you stop smoking.
• You are surprised at the ease with which you now stop smoking.
• You're taking so much pride and pleasure at stopping smoking.
• You are amazed at how easily you now stop smoking.
• You're feeling so much pride in being able to stop smoking.
• You're feeling better.
• And looking better.
• You will take an interest in your appearance.
• You will feel increased vitality.
• You will take an interest in your own shape and fitness.
• You will feel younger and fitter.
• Now a lot of people substitute eating more food or hair twiddling or nail biting or whatever else when they stop smoking but instead you are gaining a greater control of your life.
• Instead of substituting food by overeating you're taking an interest in your health.
• The thing that you're substituting for that old habit of smoking is a sense of pride in the way you look, the way you feel, and the way you smell.
• The thing you do instead of smoking is to breathe with your diaphragm to bring about, and maintain,

feelings of relaxation, calmness and control.

Allow yourself to drift deeper and deeper still now. You're more and more relaxed and you're feeling good. You feel that all the tension has gone from your body and your mind and all of you is just totally calm and relaxed.

In a moment I will count from ten down to zero. Every time I count you will feel more and more relaxed so that by the time I reach 'zero' you will be completely calm. More calm than you have ever been before. More relaxed than you have ever been before.

Ten....you are feeling sleepier and you just want to relax.
Nine...drifting deeper and deeper.
Eight...feeling so lazy, so lethargic.
Seven...letting your muscles sag completely as you drift deeper and deeper down.
Six...relaxing more and more.
Five...feeling calm, feeling sleepier and sleepier.
Four....deeper and deeper.
Three....So deep, so calm, so peaceful.
Two....just letting go, drifting deeper and deeper.
One....So relaxed....so relaxed.
Zero....Just letting go....drifting into a deep, deep sleep where nobody needs anything. Where all there is to do is relax.

I want you now to imagine a measuring ruler in front of you. And the scale on that ruler is from your age directly in front of you reducing down to zero years old.

Now look back along that scale, count back along that scale until you can see or imagine yourself as a very young person. Count back along that scale until you can see or imagine yourself as a non smoker.

Now look along that scale until you can see or imagine

the point when you had your first cigarette. See yourself taking that first puff and as an adult ask yourself if you are proud that the person you see there is taking their first smoke.

**(This part is important. Allow time in your recording to ask the questions that follow and to give answers.)**

Now ask that person why they are going to smoke. Ask them and listen to the answers. Now tell that person why they are wrong in thinking in the way they are. Give them your advice. Tell them why, in your opinion, they should remain a non smoker, how they will benefit from being a non smoker.

Now I want you to remember who that person is. It is **you** at a very young age, an age when you were happy to live for the moment. Now explain to that person that there will come a point when you will become a non smoker for ever-more, a point at which there is more to live for than smoking, a point when you will realise how silly, how expensive, how health threatening, how socially embarrassing smoking is.

The young person will ask you when that time is, hear that person ask you when that time will come, and tell that person the date that you became a non smoker.

Now hear that young person tell you how proud they are of you for having become a non smoker. How proud they are that you have become a non smoker. Remember, that young person is you, that young person is you. Now hear yourself tell yourself as you are today, how proud you are of yourself that you have become a non-smoker, how proud you are of yourself.

Now move along the scale until you reach today, until you reach now.

Now take a deep breath in, and as you breathe out, relax and open your mind completely to accept the suggestions that I will now give you, and the suggestions that I will now give you about being a non-smoker will stay in your mind and you will act on them.

You are free of withdrawal symptoms because every time you lit a cigarette before, and you took a deep inhalation, you were flushing away the build up of stale gases in the lower parts of your lungs. That made you feel better. However, what was happening was that you were using the cigarette to breathe correctly. From now on you will use deep abdominal breathing to flush away those stale gases and, as a result you will feel better. What you thought were withdrawal symptoms in the past were those gases going back into your bloodstream. Now that you know how to breathe effectively, you will feel better whenever you take those deep breaths into the lower parts of your lungs. As a result:

**(More suggestions.)**

• You are amazed at the ease with which you stop smoking.
• You are so pleased at the ease with which you stop smoking.
• You're feeling better as a non-smoker.
• You're feeling much better.
• You are healthier.
• You're feeling your whole body respond to the new non-smoking person that you are.
• You are feeling better.
• You are feeling better about yourself.
• You are so pleased that you have been able to become a non-smoker so easily.
• Your health will be better.
• You will look better.
• More attractive.
• You will feel your whole body respond to the new

103

non-smoking person that you are.
- Your hair smells fresh.
- Your breath smells fresh and you are so proud of your ability to become a non-smoker.
- This pleases you so much.
- And people you meet with notice how much fresher you look and smell and they are be proud of you.
- People at home notice how much fresher you look and smell and they are proud of you.
- Your friends notice how much fresher you look and smell and they are proud of you.
- Of course there will be some people who are jealous of your ability to stop smoking.
- And if these people ask you to smoke....
- If they offer you a cigarette....
- Feel a huge sense of pride when you tell them that you are a non-smoker.
- You do smell fresher and cleaner and you feel so proud of yourself that you have stop smoking.
- Every day you will feel more and more pride at stopping smoking, more and more pride at being in control of yourself, more and more proud of being healthy.
- You find the smell of cigarettes and cigars and pipes terrible and you know that you have the confidence to refuse any of them because you are a non-smoker.
- You feel so much pride that you have stop smoking.
- And every time you smell the clothes and hair of a smoker and you realise how bad it is the sense of pride that you have in being a non-smoker will grow.
- And as time passes you will find that sense of pride growing bigger and bigger still at having stopped smoking.
- Instead of substituting food by overeating you are taking a greater interest in your health.
- You're breathing in a deep and beneficial way.
- You're taking an interest in your appearance.
- You're feeling increased vitality.
- You're taking an interest in your own shape and fitness.

- You already feel younger and fitter.

Now just relax.

Take a deep breath and relax. Just continue to enjoy this feeling of calm.

Imagine now that you are still just lying on that beach in the warm sun, relaxed, happy and proud that you are a non-smoker.

Now bring to mind again that time scale and, this time, look ahead for one year. When you reach a year from now I want you to look at yourself. I want you to see yourself, and to see yourself as a healthy non smoker. You see that your body shape is as you want it to be and you look good.

Now imagine that you can sniff yourself and feel so proud at how good you smell, how fresh you smell. Now imagine you can somehow see inside your own body and look at your lungs. Just go inside your own body and look at your lungs. See how pink they are. How happy they are. How efficiently they are working. Now look at your heart. You see that it is pumping perfectly. Imagine you can feel your heart and lungs saying, thank you for becoming a non smoker. Hear them saying thank you for making our job so much easier. This makes you feel so proud.

Now return to today and just continue to relax. All the suggestions that I gave you about being a non-smoker will stay in your mind and you will act on them.

Remember the breathing methods that you have learnt. You remember to use them. They help you, it is the feeling of calmness that you thought you were getting from the cigarettes.

Now just relax and feel peaceful.

In a moment I will ask you count from 1 to 5 in your mind to yourself. When you reach the number 5 you will wake up, open your eyes and you will be feeling alert and will be feeling good.

You will be so proud that you are now a non smoker. Start counting from 1 to 5 now.

**(CONGRATULATIONS)**

# CHAPTER THIRTEEN

# WEIGHT CONTROL

## THE SECRET LANGUAGE

PEOPLE IN WESTERN SOCIETY are under huge body-image stress. Our ideals of looking good are imposed by movie makers and media superstars. We are bombarded by images of people on television, in films and magazines.

Career progression seems to be related to personal appearance. Fashionable clothes and fashionable body shapes are highly valued, highly prized and often highly priced. People feel that they need to look good to succeed in the giant business corporations of the world.

Children are persuaded to look and act as young adults. They are given role models who are pop-stars and super-models. They are the celebrities who follow the ideas that they need to 'look good' to be successful. Sadly, this usually translates as being thin and sexy. Youngsters attend schools that are the meeting places for youth. They are also crucibles for ideals and criticisms. Unfortunately, they can also be the high-pressure boiler houses where peer pressure and bullying take place.

Set against the huge marketing effort for high energy foods and drinks, items that are often high in sugar and fat, the drive to be thin is enormous and difficult. Those who 'succeed' too well risk eating disorders such as anorexia and bulimia. Those who 'fail' can be seduced into obesity. We have been fed a rich diet of the perfect body shape. But in whose eyes?

Our doctors are best placed to set optimum weights for heights. Actuaries, people who assess life risk factors are able to identify the dangers of smoking and obesity.

Power, sexual and social imaging should be secondary but, unfortunately, short term satisfaction seems to have replaced the need to be healthy.

We have artificially changed our body images by dieting. We have antagonised the systems that have kept us alive for millennia.

Now I will describe a weight and shape control method that really works. Perhaps you have heard those claims many times before! Yet, if any of them were true then you would not be reading this chapter now.

The method has nothing to do with dieting or calorie counting. It has nothing to do with fads such as elimination diets, nor eating only protein or carbohydrates or high fibre foods. Those methods can be antagonistic to the natural shape control systems that we have and often end up with the opposite results to those you intended.

Rather than being a new method, this weight and shape control system is as old as humans and other animals. It is something that is built into us from birth. Our own internal resources can be utilised. Until now, we have ignored them. We have failed to recognise the systems that we have. This section will explain how and why your mind and body can work together to help you. It will show you what to do to use them.

The only miracle is the wonder of your bodily processes. The only new thing is finding out how to work with, rather than against, the intrinsic resources that you have. We have been born with the tools we need, but we seem to have lost the handbook. The following is a fresh copy of that manual.

I will show you how to use the psychology and biology of your mind and body to achieve the shape that you want. The methods are safe, easy and effective. Above all, they are natural. They have worked wonderfully well with many people. Be confident that they will also work for you.

We do have body images, blueprints or what are called 'set weights', a biological term used for animals whose weights or shapes do not change. This is the secret language of success. Recognising that we do have a sense of shape is the key to a healthier and happier life so please enjoy yours.

Note. Most of the references are made for women. Of the thousands of people that I have helped to lose weight, most have been female. Therefore I am not being sexist in any way. I am simply making the narrative easier to use. The method works equally well for men.

## YOUR BODY-SHAPE-BLUEPRINT

The body-shape blueprint is exactly what it sounds like. Throughout human history our bodies and minds have worked together to establish and maintain the body shapes that optimise our chances of survival. The most variable factor in this body-shaping is the amount of fat that is stored.

Regrettably, the basic shapes that we are given have been corrupted by the abundance of food that exists in modern life and by our attempts to control how we look. We view fat as an enemy that has to be eliminated. Ironically, when we fight our reserves of fat then we encourage our systems to store even more. The battle that we start within our minds and bodies is one that we find difficult, if not impossible, to win.

However, before we progress with the techniques, we need to explore our biology.

## Homeostasis

Our bodies are wonderful systems. We maintain balances in many ways. The process is called **homeostasis,** which means 'steady state'. For example, our body temperatures are kept within a very narrow range. We use internal, rather than external, senses to maintain that balance.

We know that on a hot day we sweat. When that sweat evaporates it cools our skin which helps to cool our blood. On a cold one we divert blood from our extremities so that we do not lose heat. If prolonged, this can cause frostbite on our feet and hands. We shiver so that muscular activity warms our blood. These things happen as a response to outside conditions but the outside temperature is only relevant to our internal temperature in terms of what needs to happen in order to maintain our 37°C.

Our homeostatic systems also control the density of our blood, the mix of gases in our blood, blood pressure, sexual drive, sugar levels, thirst, appetite and much more.

Less well known is that our weight, or more exactly our shape, is also maintained within a small range. If we can imagine that we possess a 'blue-print' for shape, then it helps. To use computer terms, we can accept that we possess a 'virtual' thermometer for our temperature, and a virtual chemical laboratory for hormones. To advance the idea of a 'virtual' body-shape-blueprint is reasonable.

Our 'blue-prints' keep our shapes the same, give-or-take a few pounds, until interfered with by life circumstances, social influences and by our attempts to consciously lose weight by starvation methods. Obsessive calorie counting and rapid diets antagonise our well adjusted systems.

110

This maintenance of our bodily systems takes place in a small part of the brain called the **hypothalamus**. This brain structure, roughly the size of a walnut, receives sensory information from the body. It then regulates the body to ensure stability.

**Metabolism** is the name for the chemical reactions that take place in the body that use nutrients to provide energy and to make, or replace, body materials. Metabolism increases during pregnancy, menstruation and the consumption of food. It also speeds up during activity and when there are excess thyroid hormones. It decreases as we get older and during starvation.

The hypothalamus is involved in metabolism. It has affects on levels of hormones such as insulin, thyroxin and leptin. Leptin, from the Greek *leptos* meaning thin, was discovered as recently as 1994 and relates to the fat mass of the body.

These hormones, and others, are associated with appetite, weight control and metabolism. They are all involved with fat mass and body weight, something referred to as 'set-weight' for all animals, strangely, with the exception of humans. It is the ideal weight, or shape, for each individual. All creatures have internal body images that are established and regulated. You can watch 100,000 wildebeests run through an African plain and they all look the same. Nobody has interfered with their ideas about fashionable shapes.

Of course, we humans are animals. We also have 'set weights' but I will refer to them as the **body-shape-blueprint** as we need to develop a conscious awareness of our body shapes.

The term, weight, is measured in pounds and kilos. They are artificial concepts that have little relevance to our body shape. To demonstrate this point, if you weigh yourself in pounds, convert that number to stones or kilograms, these new numbers mean very little to you.

Our blueprints have been inherited from our primeval ancestors, but we like to think that we can eradicate our natures with conscious resolve. Our awareness of our shapes is the root of our weight problems. We interfere with our outer appearances to the detriment of our inherent systems. Rather than dieting or calorie counting we need to address our blueprints.

Naturally, different species will have a range of shapes according to seasons and locations. Polar bears put on huge reserves of fat to sustain them through hibernation, but by the time spring appears they are light enough to hunt their prey again. However, their extremes are within a set range. And those variations account for a very changeable habitat.

It is interesting to note that overweight wild animals are rarely seen. This is for three main reasons:

1. First of all, overweight animals are less able to run away from predators.

2. Secondly, underweight animals will be weak and unable to fight off their hunters.

3. Thirdly, and of most relevance to humans, their body blueprints have not been interfered with by concepts of fashion, and therefore remain unchanged. We are aware that domestic animals will become overweight when fed as if they are human.

The first two reasons are linked to survival, and that is the one fundamental purpose of life. We need to survive in our own generation and the next. For hundreds of thousands of years we have lived among our predators and prey. We have lived in a variety of lands and climates, and still do. Yet we are soft bodied, we lack horns, fangs, claws and scaly armour. How have we

112

stayed alive as a species? The answer is that we are magnificent at surviving and our systems for keeping us alive are perfect.

Yet, tragically, we have an enemy that is all pervading and highly dangerous. It is called civilisation and it threatens us and our offspring. It even endangers our planet. Civilisation is merely a thin veneer over the real animal inside but it has stopped us from hunting for our food. It has tied us to telephones, televisions, desks and computer keyboards.

Stress, anxiety and panic disorders arise from our other main survival system. The 'fight-or-flight' response or the adrenaline rush is one which also causes modern people huge problems. It kicks into action in a world that perceives threats as emotional as well as physical entities. Once more, hormones play a major part in the initiation of this survival reaction. Yet again, at the centre of the response lies the hypothalamus, our little guardian. And there are also very natural ways in which we can mediate the 'fight-or-flight' response when we work with our systems rather than against them.

**Before it became excessive, fat WAS good for us**

Way back in time, in our cave-dwelling years, humans needed to store fat for the long winters and for when times would be hard. Men needed fat to sustain them during a long and unsuccessful hunting trip. Mothers needed stores of fat in order to survive and suckle their children. Children restricted the time available for mothers to search for food.

Above all, the need to survive famines was paramount. Fifty thousand years ago, life was hard and perilous. Believe it or not, the body's ability to store fat is about survival, and we have been good at surviving as a species until our whole pattern of life was changed by imposed standards of attractiveness, fashion and chic.

The natural systems that have kept us alive for hundreds of thousands of years seem to work against us in modern times. That is mostly because we work against them. We are a species that has lived, pretty much unchanged, for hundreds of thousands of years. The great thing is that we are still here. We have survived, and fat is part of that success.

Those primeval roots are still a major part of us. When reference is made to humans as primeval beings, offence is sometimes taken. Rather than meaning that we are primitive, the word means that we have not changed our physiology very much in the last fifty thousand years. That is something that we should be proud of. We got it right back then and we have stayed on this planet to the point where we now dominate every plant, animal and mineral that exists.

If you doubt our primeval natures, consider why we sleep at higher levels than those in which we are awake. Bedrooms usually offer better views of the outside scenery than rooms on the ground floor, yet it seems that we feel the unconscious need to be off the ground to avoid nocturnal predators.

During the warmer months we barbeque our food on an open hearth outside the house. That overcooked, often burnt, food is desirable because it has been cooked as it was in our cave-dwelling days. On vacation we wallow at waterholes (swimming pools) or at the edge of the sea in loincloths (swim-suits). We throw rocks at each other in the shape of Frisbees or balls. Need I go on to make the point?

The key to weight and shape control lies in the recognition of our successful human roots. We are then able to accept an understanding of our blue-prints and our potential to change them.

## WHY OUR BLUEPRINTS CHANGE

Throughout history fat has helped to keep us alive. It has acted as insulation. It has been an energy store. It has enabled us to endure famines. It has been our savings account for rainy days.

Money has the very much the same purpose that fat used to, but we have retained the need to store fat as well. We can never have too much money but we can have too much fat.

When we look back fifty thousand years to how we were when our unconscious minds and our bodies took responsibility for our well-being, then we can see some startling facts about modern approaches to weight and shape. As with all other mammals, we have the natural capability to fluctuate through the seasons of the year. Other animals acquire stores of fat before winter in order to survive hibernation. We had to do the same, but as we did not hibernate our reserves were regulated within our need to be mobile enough to scavenge during the lean months.

Imagine, for a moment, a woman sitting at the entrance to her cave fifty thousand years ago. Her shape was controlled more by her need to stay alive rather than by any thoughts of health or fashion. She probably gave very little conscious thought to her shape. She had no mirrors, scales or comprehension of her personal weight.

Only in more modern times would external ideals about shape arrive from fashion magazines, films, television and peer pressure. So, way back in time, our cave woman would have been content.

When winter arrived and food became short then she would have relied upon her body fat to remain alive, and if she had children, to keep them alive with her breast milk. She was unable to nip out to the local supermarket to top up her larder. Had the winter progressed for longer than usual then she would starve. A famine would have begun. If she survived, by the time that food became available again, she would have been very thin.

When food became more plentiful then she would have had the urge to eat to replace the fat she had lost. The crisis would have changed her blueprint to make her larger so that if another food shortage happened she would be better able to survive. Her fat store was now greater, or in modern terminology, she had become fatter.

Please do not assume that this only applied tens of thousands of years ago. This pattern applied until very recently. We can consider how similar they are to the life-styles in the 19th century for Europeans and for the American settlers. They even apply in the poorer countries of today. In the Western world, food only became very abundant a good few years after the Second World War.

It is this very survival system of storing fat that makes people put on weight after going on a diet. This is at the root of the classic 'yo-yo' dieting process. Our brains, our minds, cannot differentiate between a life threatening famine and the self-imposed diet. A diet is beyond the remit of the older parts of the brain. The effect of a diet is to evoke an unconscious feeling of danger, the famine response. The biological answer is to increase reserves of fat in order to ensure survival.

**Why mothers put on weight**

In those early days of human existence people did not have refrigerators or deep-freezers. They had no supermarkets down the valley. Everything our forebears ate had to be found by themselves. The one safe place

116

in which food would have been stored was in mother. She had the capacity to store food as fat that could be expressed back to the children as breast milk. It is likely that her children would have used her in the same way modern children use a vending machine!

100 years ago, Leonid Brezhnev, the ex-general secretary of the Soviet Union is reported to have been breastfed by his mother to the age of 5 because he was a sickly child and times were hard. Even today there would be no choice for a mother in breast feeding her offspring or have them die from starvation.

## Why mothers finish food left on their children's' plates

Mothers seem to have an urge to finish leftover food from their children. Does this strike a chord with you? The vast majority of mothers of young children seem to feel the drive to clear plates, or to cook a little extra when feeding their children. Way back in time there was nowhere to store food for the next day without risk of contamination except in mother. She could then give the stored fat back as milk. Never be revolted, it is a sign of our wonderful heritage.

## Why men and women store fat in different bodily locations

When we look back at primeval life-styles, we can see why men and women store fat in different bodily locations. Men as the hunters of larger prey needed extra mobility to escape the other predators and to catch their own food. They would have stored fat on their fronts and backs. It is always strange to see how thin the legs of overweight men are when spotted on a beach.

Women would have been situated more around the homestead in order to guard their children. They would have foraged and hunted locally. Therefore women could store fat in a circle around their bodies from the chest to the thighs as they needed less mobility and were the source of milk for their infants.

## Why grandparents put on weight

Fifty thousand years ago as men grew older, their sons would have done the hunting. As men aged they were less able to track animals for the long periods of time that had to be invested. The older men would have grown bigger to have an advantage of power through force. Look at families of gorillas to see how this happens. Men would have localised themselves and would have had a role in the protection and education of their grandchildren. They would have also been at risk when food became scarce.

Until recently, grandmothers tended to put on weight as they grew older. Perhaps in our caves the older women were at the back of the pecking-order after the children, mother, father and her mate if he had survived. She was probably the only female in the family who could not have more children in a crisis. If grandmother had a good store of fat then she was more likely to survive a famine if one happened.

## Why we comfort eat

Back in our old family, when the weather started to turn colder then the need to store food as fat would have become greater. The nights becoming longer and the subsequent gloominess made us turn to foods that contained sugars and fats. Call it general anxiety, or the need for greater security, but the drive to consume food grew. If we take the phrase 'comfort eating' and re-name it 'security eating', then the picture becomes clearer. It is the result of the knowledge that winter was drawing closer. They were the times when food became scarcer.

This is why people will lose weight and then regain it quickly after circumstances such as a separation, divorce, bereavement and so on. Fat reserves are then added in case it happens again. This relates to the loss of a hunter/gatherer and it stimulates the need to save fat to last out the future days of possible hardship.

## Why overweight people are often fast eaters

Back in time, when we went out and found food growing on bushes or when we had killed an animal, we had two main urges. The first was to consume our bounty straight away because if we went back later then other animals would have eaten what had been left.

The second was to get out of there as quickly as possible before we became prey to the predators that were also hunting for food. So when we eat quickly we tend to consume more. The stomach is a very flexible thing that will expand to carry whatever is pushed into it.

When we eat slowly we put our minds back into the cave where there was little to eat or do. The moral of the story is to slow down when eating. This is the secret of Mediterranean diets where families will enjoy a long, slow main meal at lunchtime rather than rush through a big dinner in the evening.

## A modern perspective

The need to survive still exists. We worry about our work, our families, old age, our pensions, health-care, war, terrorism and just about everything. Our civilised ways have not stopped us from having misgivings about life. In our modern lands of plenty, we store food as fat as if we had to exist for months on our own resources.

Obesity is a contemporary ailment. Rather than using our survival mechanisms to control our weight and shape, we have antagonised our systems by dieting and calorie counting. We strive for the shapes that we are told we should desire with methods that seem to backfire. It is tragic that, until now, we have ignored the tools that we possess already. The successes with the body-shape blueprint method have been achieved by working with the biology and psychology of the human body, rather than evoking a response from dieting which works against the objective of losing weight.

## MODERN INFLUENCES THAT CAN CAUSE WEIGHT GAINS

### Social influences

People who have been abused may put on weight for protection. Bully victims want to be 'bigger' to avoid physical hurt. We are unable to make ourselves taller, but we can make ourselves wider. Fat may be perceived as armour against punches. Excess fat can also be seen as a repellent of sexual advances.

At the other extreme, the refusal to grow can be an attempt to cling onto childhood, those 'safer' times. This has a bearing on the low-weight problems associated with anorexia and bulimia. These issues are outside the scope of this book and are best helped with specific therapies.

### Like father, like son

Size, as in the build and height of a person, is almost certainly to do with genetics and nurture. However, the amount of fat that is carried by a person is probably more to do with other influences. Overweight people blame genetics as a 'get-out' clause. If a person's parents are overweight, they can blame their ill-fortune on their ancestors and they will be less mentally able to tackle their own size problems.

It might be worth considering that in our survival make-up we might have a predisposition to copy the shapes of those people around us. If they are carrying a lot of fat, then perhaps it indicates that they live in a high risk valley, in primeval terms. Therefore it would seem to make sense that we imitate their shapes to further our own chances of continued existence.

I beg your pardon, but primeval times are over.

We live in times of plenty. As a result of world trading we do not even have seasonal variations in the foodstuffs available every day of the year. Our need to store food is negated by modern methods of refrigeration and farming. If you and your family are overweight, move your minds to the fertile valley in which you already live. The famine will never happen. Stop worrying! Change your blueprint to suit the lush, fertile and abundant valley in which you exist.

In short, lose weight if you are too fat. In current times, this is far more relevant to your survival.


**Bigger is worse rather than better**

Our culture is based on acquisition. We want bigger houses, cars, bank balances and so on. This desire for more even has a food-orientated description; greed. We live in a commercial society where you can 'buy-one-and-get-one free'. We have offers that encourage us to buy larger portions of 'fries'. We have 'all-you-can-eat' restaurants. And this pushing of food and excessive eating feeds the slimming market.

Think of those offers and promotions as nothing more than an attempt to take your money whilst making you fatter. And when you are fat, there are plenty of people who will take your money by offering diets to help you slim. Remember that fast food is more food, eaten quickly. Bigger is seldom better in terms of health. Being skinny is rarely better either, so starvation diets should be avoided. Rapid results often lead to weight gain. The best solution is to strive to be normal, neither too big, nor too thin.

## Bingeing and comfort eating

We have already established that anxiety relates to eating habits such as bingeing and comfort eating. The famine response may be evoked when times seem stressful. Bingeing and comfort eating occur when people feel that hard times are happening, or are coming. If this applies to you, then you know what I mean! Bingeing is similar to primeval feasting. Feasting is a feature within our history. Perhaps finishing food before it went bad, perhaps sharing the outcome of a hunt. They were all to add fat to the personal store in anticipation of 'leaner' days. We still do it in mid-winter to this day, but we call it Christmas or something else.

This leaves nibbling. Nibbling through the day is the way in which other primates consume their food. Those urges are still with us. Very few animals eat a regular set of three meals per day. We do. However, when we combine set meals with nibbling we confuse our systems.

## The urge to eat sugar and fat

In primeval days sweet foods were rare. Fruits never seem to have the sweetness of modern confectionary. The fat on wild prey animals tends to be less than modern farmed animals. Older civilisations such as the Kalahari Bushmen will risk life and limb in search of honey. But that is a rare treat rather than something to be found in sweet-shops. In our days of plenty we seem to crave excesses of the foods that were necessary fifty thousand years ago but which are superfluous today.

The mind is a sophisticated thing and is very different to a computer. Logic works in a computer but the human mind runs on emotion as well as logic. We need to make the mind and body feel safe enough to reduce the fat stockpile. In our minds we need to move to that better valley.

## FOLLIES OF CALORIE COUNTING AND DIETS

The unconscious systems of the body and mind rank survival higher than a conscious desire to be fashionable. Weight and shape-control are parts of a huge industry. Profit is the goal. Sometimes, this can be at the expense of health. Some industry fat-cats want to convert the dream of weight loss into fat profits.

If just one successful diet had been developed then there would only be one diet that was used by everybody. Has anybody ever got dieting/calorie counting right?

We seem to lack the ability to maintain our shapes in accordance with our conscious desires. Our innate ability to control our body shape is one of the survival systems that have kept us going for all our history, until recently.

In order to work WITH the natural systems of the mind and body we must break down some of the main assumptions used in traditional dieting and weight control methodology.

### Why calorie counting does not help

The major way in which your body shape is controlled is by metabolism. Some people will burn food at a higher rate than others in order to maintain their blueprint. Other people will burn food at a lower rate.

According to studies into appetite regulation, the daily

intake of food is highly variable and correlates poorly with energy usage. Despite this, over long periods of time body weights are usually stable in most adults.

Going back fifty thousand years again, it would have been pointless to burn 1500 calories per day during a famine. Soon the reserves of fat would have been burnt off and our cave dwellers would have died. It is much more likely that in order to hold onto body shape, or reserves of fat, metabolism would have slowed.

In modern times, when a person reduces their calorie intake during a diet, then the metabolism slows to maintain the blueprint shape as much as possible. This is called 'metabolic shift'. This is why dieters will become lethargic and miserable. Their metabolism has slowed to ensure the lowest possible usage of stored energy.

The mind and body are screaming for the things that will replace the fat loss. The best thing to replace lost fat is fat! That is why dieters get cravings for certain products. They are, of course, sugar and fat. And then there is the ultimate mix of the two, chocolate.

We all know people who can eat the whole candy section of a supermarket and remain thin. We also know those who only eat a lettuce leaf and seem to gain a pound. This has more to do with the movement of metabolic rates to maintain the blueprint than calorific intake. When you set your blueprint shape, then you can trust your system to achieve it.

We are different to steam trains! The energy from a certain amount of coal will fuel a boiler for a certain distance. That is measurable. We are humans with a system that works to keep us alive. If we reduce our fuel intake then we will reduce the rate at which we burn it.

## Why dieting can be counter-productive

There is a joke about a two page diet book giving a system that should work. On page one it says, 'Eat less, and take more exercise'. On page two it says, 'See page one!'

Reducing food intake only works when it is recognised by the mind and body as beneficial to survival. Therefore, when slow weight reduction at approximately seven pounds per month is translated as a movement towards a beneficial blueprint shape, it is accepted.

When weight loss is rapid it evokes the 'famine-response'. Your system will be driven to add reserves of fat rather than to risk exposure to starvation.

The same applies to elimination diets. We are omnivores. We eat anything and everything. By doing so, we achieve a balance of nutrients, vitamins and minerals. When we eliminate certain food groups, we signal danger yet again. We are impelled to consume those things that our systems feel we are missing in order to sustain homeostasis.

We are not the only modern species that has become fatter. The animals that we farm are deliberately fattened so that there is more weight per lamb, pig, cow or chicken. This means that there is more fat to be consumed in meat in the twenty-first century than in the many thousands of years ago before farming became driven to produce 'bigger and fatter'.

A wild deer will be leaner because it has to compete for scarce food resources, and as mentioned earlier it would have been at a disadvantage if it were slow in escaping. As farming is an industry, the extra fat that is produced has to be disposed of in the food chain. Those excess fats are found in manufactured foods. It is found in pastries, pies, burgers and savoury snacks. Fats are used to cook foods such as French fries. Fat is added to our food in subtle ways. Not only do we have more food in our times, but we have a higher proportion of fat in our diets.

The same point can be made about sugar. The sources of sweetness in our history were fruits and perhaps, more perilously, honey. Bees want to keep their external stores of sugars.

Now we have used sugar canes and beet to manufacture sugar which is used in our drinks, confections and as an additive to many foods. The high consumption of sugar is contributing to the huge increase in diabetes. The hypothalamus and pancreas have been over-burdened to the point where they are unable to cope.

So fats and sugars are a danger in excess. Yet fats and sugars are widely used and available. When they are eaten by overweight people they cause 'guilt-trips'. Those feelings of remorse add to anxiety. Anxiety leads to comfort/security eating. That leads to an increase of fat and sugar intake. Additional sugar and fat lead to 'guilt-trips' and so on.

So people go on crash diets and count calories in an attempt to slim. The yo-yo dieting cycle kicks in. More weight, more guilt, more food and more fat. The vicious circle is complete. And when obesity and diabetes and heart disease enter onto the scene, the circle is very vicious indeed.

There is a way to break that pattern. We need to look to our history, psychology and biology. We need to use the good sense that we have been given

**USING OUR SENSES**

We need to address the issues of weight and shape

from a different perspective to that of counting calories and fad diets. We need to use the natural resources that we have.

We are able to control our body shapes rather than provoking the responses that work against them. By working **with** our inherent systems, we can encourage weight loss in the medium to longer term.

Although this will seem like a new approach to weight control, it is hundreds of thousands of years old. Only since we started interfering with our natural systems through the use of dieting has the need to regain control of our internal weight and shape mechanisms become of paramount importance.

We are told that we have five senses, namely sight, hearing, touch, smell and taste. They are the ones that we are familiar. They are for becoming aware of the world outside our bodies. They allow us to become acquainted with our environment.

We actually have more than those five. They are the inner senses. They are the ways in which our bodies experience and regulate themselves internally. For example, we have a sense of balance, kinaesthesia. This is the sense that tells you which way-up you are. It is the one that gives you a feeling of movement, direction and orientation when you are in an aircraft.

Then there is another sense that is used in re-setting your body-shape-blueprint. It is called **proprioception**, from **proprius** meaning 'one's own' and per**ception**, which gives you information about where you are in space. It gives you an internal perspective. This is your sense of proportion.

**Getting to know what proprioception is.**

Please do these exercises. It is important that you

become familiar with this sense of bodily feedback. They involve closing your eyes, so please remember the instructions or have somebody read them to you.

## Exercise 1.

Extend the first finger on your right hand, extend your arm to the side, close your eyes and then touch the end of your nose with the extended digit.

Which sense did you use to find your nose? You were unable to see it, your eyes were closed. You were unable to taste, smell or hear it. You only felt it when you made contact with your nose.

This is the sense that is used as a preliminary drink-drive test by the American police. It is a sense that is relevant to weight or shape control because it is the awareness of where parts of you are in relation to the rest of you. It is easily switched into.

## Exercise 2.

Without moving or touching yourself, feel the sole of your left foot. You are sending slow nerve impulses to the sole of your foot so that you can verify its existence. Signals are then sent back to tell you that it is there. It is like using radar to detect something and then to pinpoint its location.

## Exercise 3.

Again, without moving or actually touching yourself, feel where your right hip is. Now feel where your left hip is. Now feel the space between them. This body checking is going on all the time, but at an unconscious level. However we can switch our conscious thought into it at will. We can feel our shape within our own mind. This sensory information is being fed into the hypothalamus.

## Exercise 4.

When you are ready, close your eyes. Put your hands out in front of you, palm facing palm. Now spread your hands to what you think is the distance between your hips. Then open your eyes and decide how accurate you were. This exercise necessitated you to get proprioceptive feedback and then relay it to your arms and hands. You then verified the position of your hands with an external sense, your vision.

You have now experienced the blending of the two senses that you will use to change your blue-print.

## Exercise 5.

Now, with your eyes closed and <u>without</u> touching yourself with your hands, use proprioception to feel the fat on the back of your upper arm as it is. Now feel the shape of that part of your arm as you would like it to be.

This is the insight to weight and shape control. Presume that the feedback goes into a processor, which checks against a blueprint and then changes our system to maintain our shape. This processor is your hypothalamus. Of course, we are unable to see an actual blueprint in a person's brain, but it can be seen within our mind's-eye or, for some people, felt with the mind's hand.

The good news is that we can consciously change our blueprints, and when that is done, our bodies will change their shapes.

Blueprints are re-drawn with visualisation and proprioception. You become aware of every part of your body bit by bit from the shape you are now to the shape that you would like to be, within reason. Within reason is important because the mind and body work for survival. Remember that super-model shapes are for selling clothes, rather than for copying! If you see/feel yourself at an unhealthy body shape, you run the risk of problems.

## CHANGING YOUR BLUEPRINT

The first time that you carry out this procedure, go through it slowly. Ensure that you are getting conscious feedback. When this happens, your unconscious blueprint senses are also involved.

Very soon we will embark upon a proprioception awareness routine during which we will start making the changes to your blueprint to achieve the shape that you want to be. However, there is some preliminary work that needs to be done.

| |
|---|
| COMMENCEMENT DATE: |
| CURRENT WEIGHT: |
| TARGET WEIGHT: |
| DIFFERENCE: |
| TARGET DATE *: |
| TARGET DATE 'PICTURE' ** |
| * Calculate your target date by dividing the weight difference by 7 pounds, or 3.2 kilos. This will give you the number of months in which you will achieve your target shape when you follow the instructions given on the recording. Add these months, or part months, to the commencement date to give you your target date. |
| ** Now associate that date with a real point in time. For example, a birthday, anniversary, a holiday or a season. Perhaps something like the appearance of flowers in your garden. Do whatever you can to lock in your target date to an actual point of time. |

1. First of all, write down your current weight in the grid on the next page.

2. Now write down your realistic target weight.

3. Work out the difference in pounds or kilograms.

4. You should aim to lose weight at the rate of 7 pounds, or 3.2 kilos per month. Remember that losing weight at a faster rate runs the risk of evoking the 'famine response'.

## LISTS OF FOODS TO AVOID WHEREVER POSSIBLE

On the next page there is a table for you to look at. This includes two lists of the foods that you will avoid until you have achieved your new shape. Rather than being lists of taboo foods, these are highlighted to encourage you to avoid fats and sugars. There will be times when you will be unable to refuse those foods without seeming to be rude. Maybe at a dinner party, for example. However, the fewer of the 'avoidance' foods that you eat, the easier it will be. Remember, in the past you only craved those foods because your mind and body assumed that you were losing fat as part of a famine. Now you are working WITH those systems, so it is very much easier to be free of those old cravings.

In the first column you have 'fatty foods' as a heading. Under that heading there are items such as fried foods. Most people deny that they eat fried foods, but the reality is that they do. Think of a lamb chop being grilled. It is being fried upside down so remove the fat before cooking. Then hard fats such as cheese and butter. Next savoury snacks such as crisps and their many variations that I will avoid naming by brand, savoury snacks and salted nuts. Then hidden fats such as those that are found in sauces, convenience foods, manufactured foods such as pies and take-away foods. Remember fat is cheap and heavy. It is an easy addition

131

to manufactured foods to save costs. Add any other items that you know should be on the list. Read the list and think, item by item, which foods you know you should avoid.

Now in the second column you see the heading 'sweet foods'. There you see items such as cakes, biscuits and cookies, candy and sweets, and, of course, chocolate. Add other items that you know should be on the list. Again, read the list and think, item by item, which foods you know you should avoid.

If you eat other items not mentioned in those lists, or if you drink sugary drinks or you feel that you drink too much alcohol, add these to your list of things to avoid, or limit, under the appropriate headings.

| RATHER THAN MAKING THESES FOODS 'TABOO', AVOID THEM WHERE POSSIBLE. | |
|---|---|
| **FATTY FOODS** | **SWEET FOODS** |
| Fried foods | Cakes |
| Hard cheeses | Biscuits |
| Butter | Confectionery |
| Savoury snacks | Puddings |
| Hidden fats in sauces, pastries, and fast-food. Manufactured foods such as sausages, pies and pastries. | Chocolate |
| | Ice cream |
| | |
| | |
| | |

Do the proprioception and visualisation exercises given in the next chapter each day for the first three days and then once per week until your new blueprint shape becomes reality.
They are:

1. FEELING AND SEEING YOUR NEW BLUEPRINT SHAPE. This reinforces your new body shape blueprint by communicating with your mind and body.

2. SUGGESTIONS FOR CHANGE. Read these through. Say them out loud. They give the positive affirmations that encourage an optimistic outlook.

3. MAKING LISTS OF FOODS TO AVOID WHEREVER POSSIBLE. Although you will find that you almost naturally avoid the foods on your list, it is beneficial to bolster your resolve. Reviewing the lists will give you a feeling of pride in knowing how well you are doing.

# CHAPTER FOURTEEN

## WEIGHT CONTROL ROUTINE

THE FOLLOWING ROUTINE needs to be followed once a day for the first three days and then once per week until you have achieved your target shape. The reason is that you are changing a fundamental system that is reluctant to lose reserves of fat that are considered to be important in the primeval scheme of things. It needs gentle persuasion to change. You know that in the past your blueprint would increase easily if your system felt that extra fat reserves would enhance your chances of survival.

## FEELING AND SEEING YOUR NEW BLUEPRINT SHAPE

Because you will be quiet and peaceful, it is important that you are in a safe place, free from interruption. If you need to attend to any emergency, you will be instantly alert and wide awake and able to cope.

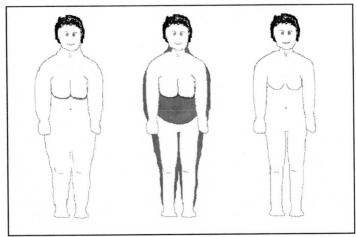

In the following steps, you will be:
1. 'Feeling' your body shape as it is. (See left sketch.)

2. 'Feeling' where the excess fat is. (Shading in the middle sketch.)

3. Then 'feel' your desired body-shape blueprint as it will be. (Right hand sketch.

**The following may be recorded as a script or read. When recording, miss out the parts in italics. Alternatively, a recording by the author is available from http://www.emp3books.com**

Settle down into a really comfortable position and let yourself relax.

The secret of relaxation rests with your breathing. Allow your breathing to expand your stomach rather than your chest. Feel the air flowing gently down into your lower abdomen and then let it flow out smoothly. Avoid inflating the chest. The muscles that pull your rib cage up are for those times when you need a high supply of oxygen in your bloodstream. Switch them off as much as possible. Use your diaphragm instead.

Do that again, feel the air flowing gently down into your lower abdomen...

...and then let it flow out smoothly. The rhythm of breathing will allow you to feel each part of your body with your mind rather than with your hands.

*Read the* (Listen to the) instructions for each part of your body one by one, and then go through the process of sensing it with your mind as it is. Get a good feeling because this is the blueprint that you possess. Remember that the 'feeling' is done with your mind, rather than with your hands. Then feel that part of your body as you would like it to be and as it is going to be.

1. Start with the top of your head; breathe in gently whilst concentrating on the top of your head. In your mind, feel its shape. Now breathe out slowly as if your

breath were taking away the excess fat on the top of your head. (In reality, the top of the head is fairly free of excess fat, but it is a good place to start so that you can work downwards.)

Now breathe into the top of your head, this time sensing it as it will be. As you breathe out, let yourself relax. 'Sense' the new shape for a slow count of five in your mind.

2. Now concentrate on your face. Feel the shape of your cheeks as they are. Feel around the eyes. Now breathe away any excess of fat. Think of your face again. This time, as you want it to be. Sense how it will be; tighter and firmer. The skin now fits closer to the facial muscles. 'Sense' the new shape for a slow count of five in your mind.

3. Now concentrate on your throat and neck as you breathe in. When you have felt your throat and neck as they are, breathe away the fat.

Now feel your throat and neck as they will be. 'Sense' the new shape for a slow count of five in your mind.

4. Now focus on the shape of the tops of your arms, especially the backs where fat covers the triceps. Breathe away the fat. Then feel your upper arms as they will be. 'Sense' the new shape for a slow count of five in your mind.

5. Now feel your chest as it is. In your mind, feel where the excess fat is. Now breathe away the fat. 'Sense' the new shape for a slow count of five in your mind.

6. Now breathe into your upper back. Feel the excess fat. When you have done that, breathe away the fat. Now 'sense' the new shape for a slow count of five in your mind.

7. Be very aware of the shape of your stomach as you breathe in slowly. This is an important area where fat is stored in men and women. Imagine you have the rolls

of fat in your hands and you are kneading them like dough. Breathe away the fat. Now sense the feeling of tightness after the fat has gone. Inhale into your stomach as it will be and experience a sense of pride as you breathe out. 'Sense' the new shape for a slow count of five in your mind.

8. Now grasp the fat on your hips and buttocks with your mind. Do as you did with your stomach. Be aware of the fat dissolving. Breathe it away gently. Feel the taut muscles that were hidden by the fat. 'Sense' the new shape for a slow count of five in your mind.

9. Now feel your thighs. Feel where they are in space, feel where the fat is. Be familiar with those masses of fat and/or cellulite. Now breathe away that fat. The fat has melted away leaving your thighs firm and toned. 'Sense' the new shape for a slow count of five in your mind. Breathe into the shape they will be, feel how much slimmer they are. Feel good.

10. Now your calves. Feel the fat covering the muscle and breathe it away. 'Sense' the new shape for a slow count of five in your mind.

11. Finally your ankles and feet. Feel them as they are and breathe away the fat. 'Sense' the new shape for a slow count of five in your mind.

12. Now sense your whole body as it will be. Sense every part of your body as you want it to be. Breathe in and out slowly and imagine that sense of pride in having achieved your ideal body shape. Breathe in and out slowly again.

13. *Now we can combine proprioception with visualisation.*

14. *Close your eyes and* Imagine yourself standing in front of a large mirror that reflects every part of you.

See yourself naked. See where that excess fat is. Now see that reflection slowly becoming the shape that you will be, the new shape that you felt as you relaxed. Feel good. Feel proud. See the new slimmer and fitter you looking back at you from the mirror.

15. Now place the image of you with that excess fat into the past. Roll your eyes to your left as you do so.

16. Now place the image of how you will be, into the future. Roll your eyes to your right as you do so.

17. Now create a space in between those images so that you will feel and see the shape that you will be the next time you do these exercises. Then you will feel that real sense of pride at the progress that you are making from the shape you were to the shape that you will be.

## SUGGESTIONS FOR CHANGE

Open your mind now to accept the positive and beneficial suggestions that follow.

1. Remember to take time when you are eating. Allow yourself to eat slowly. Enjoy the food; concentrate on the flavour and texture of each mouthful as you slowly chew your food, whether you are alone or with friends and family.

2. Wherever and whenever, sit down at a table and relax while you are eating slowly.

3. When you are choosing food to eat, remember that you have excess fats and sugars in your personal store. What you need to eat are those foods that will give you the vitamins and minerals that your body requires. Allow your body to use that excess fat that you have stored.
4. Know that you will be healthier and fitter when you have used your store of excess fat.

5. Allow your mind and body to work together to achieve your ideal shape.

6. You now find it easy to avoid fats and sugars in foods because your mind is working with your new blueprint to achieve your ideal and healthy body shape.

7. Trust in the ability of your mind and body to direct you away from fats and sugars and towards a healthier way of life.

8. Allow yourself to exercise more. Walk rather than drive, if possible. Take slightly faster steps. Feel the muscles of your body becoming toned and strong.

9. You now find the patience to carry out the 'Seeing and Feeling' exercises in order to strengthen your own sense of body image.

10. You now find the patience for your mind and body to dispose of your excess fat in a healthy way rather than rushing yourself, or by using diets that will promote your 'famine-response'.

11. Hold the image of yourself as you will be in your mind and relax. See yourself in new clothes at your target date. Associate your new body shape with that real point in time. Congratulate yourself on your success.

12. Revert to the pleasures of our ancestors. Savour the sweetness of fruit rather than consuming refined sugars.

In a moment I will ask you to count from 1 to 5 in your mind to yourself. When you reach the number 5, you will wake up; open your eyes, feeling alert and wide awake.

Start counting from 1 to 5 in your own mind...now.

# CHAPTER FIFTEEN

## TWO STORIES ILLUSTRATING THE PROBLEMS

THE FOLLOWING STORIES may seem silly at first glance, but please bear with me. The secrets for your success are contained within them. They are simply metaphors that talk to your mind in a different way.

### THE OLD TALE COMES FIRST

Let me take a family to describe the life style of people many thousands of years ago. I will give them modern names to make the story easier to tell.

*Ugg and Jugg were six year old twins. Their caring parents were Agg and Agga.*

*Agg spent all his time finding animals to bring home to his family. Sometimes he found rabbits, sometimes deer, sometimes nothing. Now and then, he would hunt with other men in order to increase the strike rate and to catch larger animals.*

*Agga foraged locally for insects, small animals, roots, nuts and berries according to the seasons. She had to be careful to avoid being eaten by hunting animals such as wolves and bears when she was occupied with her searches. Very often she would wander around with one or two friends who lived in huts nearby. When she was out looking for food, Agga's mother would keep Ugg and Jugg safe from harm. Agga's father had been killed a few years before when he had been unable to escape from a hungry bear, but that was a familiar story. Predators tend to hunt the older and less agile members of a group.*

*One winter there was a food shortage. The crops of nuts and berries had been small and there was much competition in the autumn from other animals. As the* winter arrived the large predators became more aggressive in their search for meat. There were no stores of food in those days because refrigeration had yet to be developed. The small reserves of nuts soon ran out. The twins were of the utmost priority. They were given most of the meagre supplies of food and Agga still breast fed them, using her reserves to keep the twins alive. Agg's sparse catches were consumed by him, his children and by his mate. Agga's mother was always the last in the queue and ate very little. As the famine wore on she was given nothing and had to survive on her own body reserves of fat. She became quiet, lethargic and almost zombie like. Indeed, the whole family became thin and emaciated.

Eventually the spring arrived and food became more readily available. The whole household ate and ate until they became the same shape that they had been before the famine. Then they continued to add more and more fat to their reserves in case there would be another famine in the future. Agga stored fat around her waist, her hips her arms and legs. As she browsed for food locally, her need for speed was less than Agg's who needed to be able to escape being caught more easily. So Agg stored his extra fat around his stomach to keep his arms and legs less encumbered.

The twins ate more as well. They wanted to be bigger, to be more grown-up. However, they ran around a lot, playing and converting their food to bones and muscles.

Granny ate as much as possible. She became very big. Her need was to store as much as she could. She resented being left out of the food supply and starved during the famine. She would have been the first to die had it continued. Most of the grannies in the valley were big. It seemed as if they were all in the same situation of being dispensable in the bad times.

One day the whole family moved away from this area of

risk. They climbed the hills and went through a pass into a new land that was fertile and had an abundance of food. After time passed they found that they needed smaller reserves of fat. The bad times stopped coming. It was warmer here. Their body shapes reverted to what they were before the famine in the other valley. They lived a long and healthy life in this new place.

If we could look at our family before, during and after the famine we would notice that their shapes had altered dramatically. It would be as if they had re-drawn their plans for their ideal body shapes for survival by carrying bigger reserves of fat. After moving, they all became the shapes that they needed to be less hampered by that extra load they carried. They ran around more and enjoyed their new lives.

## THE MODERN STORY COMES NEXT

John and Joan are six year old twins. Their caring parents are Jack and Jill. Jack spends all his time working to bring home money to his family. Sometimes he gets a bonus, sometimes nothing. Now and then, he works with other men in order to take on bigger contracts.
Jill drives to the local shops for meat, vegetables, nuts and berries according to the seasons. She has to be careful about being cheated when she is occupied with her searches. Very often she wanders around the shops with one or two friends who live in the houses nearby.

When she is out looking for food, Jill's mother keeps John and Joan safe from harm. Jill's father had been killed a few years before by a massive heart attack brought on by overwork, overweight and lack of exercise, but that is a familiar story. Stress tends to hunt the older and less agile members of a group.

One day Jill decided to go on a diet because she thought she was fat. Jack chose to join her because he wanted to look good like Jill's favourite film star.

They each lost eight pounds after struggling with their cravings for chocolate, cheese and salted potato crisps. The children and their grandmother lost weight as the food choices for the whole family became more and more restricted. The children were happy because they thought they looked like their favourite pop stars. Granny was upset because she felt that she was being starved.

However, their systems considered that there was a food shortage, a famine. Eventually the diet ended and food became more readily available. Much to the disappointment of Jack and Jill, the whole household ate and ate until they became the same shape that they had been before the diet. Then they seemed to be compelled to add more and more fat to their reserves in case there would be another diet, which was perceived as a famine, in the future.

Jill stored fat around her waist, hips, arms and legs. As she browsed for food locally, her mind thought that her need for speed was less than Jack's. So even though he had no need to chase prey, Jack's mind plotted to store his extra fat around his stomach to keep his arms and legs less encumbered.

The twins ate more as well. They wanted to be bigger, to be more grown-up like their super-heroes and like their parents. However, they ran around a lot, playing and converting their food to bones and muscles, but they still accumulated excess fat. They were given money which they used to buy burgers, French fries and soft drinks.

Granny ate as much as possible. She became very big. Her need was to store as much as she could. She wanted to avoid being starved as she was during the diet. She wanted to be able to enjoy this time of her life *without being deprived of chocolate, so she indulged herself.*

*Most of the grannies in the town were big. It seemed as if they were all in the same situation of being taken for granted. Their needs were considered to be of a low priority by the younger people.*

*If we could look at our family before, during and after the diet we would notice that their shapes had altered dramatically. It would be as if they had re-drawn their plans for their ideal body shapes in order to survive by carrying bigger reserves of fat. Their friends warned them about the effects of 'yo-yo' dieting. They had all done it themselves before.*

*One day Jill found a book about changing her body-shape-blueprint. She used the method and lost weight. Jack was so impressed that he used the same method and also lost weight. The twins now had new role models. They played more and ate less. They saw that food was abundant and they needed smaller fat reserves.*

*It was as if the whole family had moved to a more fertile and abundant valley and needed not to worry about the days when the snows came.*

Stories, metaphors, have an impact on the way we perceive things. By looking at the familiar in a different way we can see truths that we missed before. I hope you gained something of value from the two stories above.

## CHAPTER SIXTEEN

## SELF HYPNOSIS

## RELAXATION AND COPING TECHNIQUES

LEARNING TO RELAX is straightforward. Making the time to relax on a regular basis is the thing which causes the most problems for people. It is easy to write that you should meditate for ten minutes in the morning and for twenty minutes in the evening. People with that much time to spare should be stress-free in any event!

Therefore, the following is a realistic approach to relaxation, or self-hypnosis for people who have little time to spare. This can be done within any time-frame and in any location which is safe.

When you are relaxed, repeat suggestions and affirmations over and over in your mind. The relaxed feelings you have opened the door to your unconscious mind and you have the language to communicate with it.

## "EASY-MEDITATION."

Rather than to achieve a state of nirvana, our aim is to experience the recovery response on a regular basis in order to reduce anxiety, hence the name.

**Getting ready.** Find the most suitable place that you can. It might be an armchair, settee, bed or the floor. Equally, due to circumstances, it might be a railway carriage, your office or your car-seat in a rest stop. There should be no rules for relaxation, or time limits. Tailor your resources to your circumstances.

## HOWEVER, NEVER DO THIS WHEN DRIVING.

**The basics.**

Make yourself comfortable and safe. If you are using your car whilst parked up, for example, lock the doors. If you are in a train, ensure that any valuables that you have are secure.

**Positioning.**

Sit or lay in such a way that your body is as open as the surroundings and decency permit.
The tradition meditation position where you sit on the floor with your legs in the lotus-position is fine if you can put up with the discomfort! However, just sitting with the soles of your feet together and your knees as far apart as possible opens up the pelvic area and encourages deep abdominal breathing almost automatically. If you sit on the floor with your legs together and outstretched, you will notice how much this restricts your ability to breathe into your stomach.

If you lie or recline, make yourself as open as you are able.

Run a muscle-check. Relax your neck, shoulders and stomach. Ease out the thigh and calf muscles. Separate your ankles and open your legs as much as your situation allows. Let your arms droop down or rest them on your thighs. Open your hands.

**USING YOUR SIX SENSES.**

1. Proprioception (or mental massage)

Start with the top of your head and work down to your feet. All animals prefer to be stroked downwards than upwards. Do it to your partner, dog or cat. You will notice a difference. Concentrate on breathing slowly into your abdomen. Ignore your upper chest. That will fill on its own.

Feel, with your mind, every part of your head every time you breathe in. As you breathe out say to yourself, **"I am calm, confident and in control, now."** Or whatever positive thing you want to say to yourself.

Feel, with your mind, each part of your head including your hair, ears and nose as well as the muscles. Move down your body doing the same thing, in whichever order you like, but include every part of you. You will finish with your toes. When you get there enjoy the feeling and, if you wish, include one or more of your other senses.

2. Visualisation.

Imagine whatever gives you pleasure; a beach, a waterfall, swimming with dolphins or a person. Anything! Imagine it as a picture or as a film. Involve yourself in the scene or watch it as an observer.

3. Hearing.
Listen to imagined birdsong or waves or add your favourite music as a soundtrack. If you are travelling, listen to the rhythm of the train wheels.

4. Smelling.

Smell anything that you can. Imagine freshly cut grass, perfumes or flowers. To some, the smell of a wet dog is relaxing. Alternatively, smell the real odours around you.

5. Tasting.

Add a favourite meal or the taste of a blade of grass in your mouth.

6. Feeling.

This is the sense of feeling the world outside of us. The

textures, temperatures and shapes of things, real or imaginary.

This process of focusing thoughts onto pleasant things takes us away from the worries that haunt anxious people and puts us into a safe environment where the recovery response takes over. You relax for as long you have time to do so. For some it will be twenty minutes, for others two. There are no rules. The only thing that is important is that you do it.

## RELAXING WITH REAL EXPERIENCES

Our memories work with associations. The above exercise brings about relaxation by using the imagination with associations. We can reverse the process by using real objects to stimulate pleasant memories of relaxing events. The following are examples of things that may be used to help relaxation.

1. Proprioception.

This can be anything from dancing to Tai Chi. Movement is relaxing. Feel, with your mind, where your limbs are located in space when you move.

2. Visualising.

Look at landscapes, pictures or photographs that have pleasant connotations. Draw, even if you feel that you lack the talent.

3. Hearing.
Listen to recordings that inspire images. Listen to music, birdsong or wind-chimes. Hear children laughing. Listen to what appears to be silence and find sounds within it.

4. Smelling.

Gently sniff foods, spices, flowers. Grade them. Find

categories and rank them in order of preference.

5. Tasting.

Roll foodstuffs and drinks around in your mouth like a gourmet or wine taster. Define the differences between sweet and sour. Determine the ingredients used in the things that you eat.

6. Feeling.

Touch and feel the different textures of cloth. Model clay. Feel the different wall coverings in your house. Caress plants and/or pets.

## ROLE MODELLING

Become a method actor. Pretend that you are acting out the role of a confident person, free of stress and problems. You find role models everywhere. There are people that you admire. Copy their posture, their ways of walking, talking and breathing. You find them in real life, television and films. Watch politicians making speeches.

Admire actors in demanding parts. These successful types are acting out their lives. They were born in the same way as you and me, but they have dressed themselves in the behavioural costumes of what they want to be.

Do the same. What happens is that the fantasy gives an escape from the negative way in which you regarded yourself. It shows you that when you act a character, you become that style of person. You give yourself positive experiences, which you can grow from. You change your approach from running and hiding to that of control.

The main essence of self-hypnosis is that of occupying the conscious mind to the extent where it stops from being judgemental about the suggestions you want to pass to your unconscious. The exercises above are free of instructions to 'act-out' being hypnotised as you think it should look. You can do that if it helps, but instead, most of the time, distract your conscious mind. Prepare suggestions carefully and make them when you feel relaxed and receptive. It is as if you make an eavesdropper sit in a soundproof room while you talk to a confidante, free from interruption or interference.

# CHAPTER SEVENTEEN

# HOW TO HYPNOTISE

SO YOU WANT TO KNOW the secrets of hypnosis! In one word, compliance.

The words with which compliance is achieved are the secret ones because they contain instructions within their meanings. In the same way that negatives in speech and thought may be created by using words that become counter productive, so we are able to use words that bring people onto our team.

## Conditional outcomes

We have discovered that some words such as 'if...then' often make negative conditional outcomes. So it stands to reason that when we use positive conditional terms we can create compliance; for example 'as you...then'.

Let me give examples:
'As you read this part of the book then you will find that the information stays in your mind'. Compare that sentence with, 'if you read this part of the book you will find that the information stays in your mind'. Now you are thinking, what is the difference?

The first sentence is about you being told about a positive outcome that will happen as you do something. The 'doing' is implied. The second is telling you what to do. You are able to reject the request. From childhood we have disliked being told what to do. "How dare he tell me what to do and what will happen when I do it?" Yet we also learnt that there are some positive conditions that rewarded us. "When you tidy your bedroom I will give you some sweets."

## Choice

Another way to gain compliance is to offer choice. In selling, choice is used to get a decision. It is known as the 'tea or coffee close'. This implies that you would like a drink. All you have to do is choose which one. If you ask, 'would you like a drink?' then the answer could be 'yes' or 'no'.

## When?

Lock an outcome into the present tense. For example, 'as you breathe gently then you <u>are</u> feeling more and more relaxed.' This is far more effective than 'as you breathe gently, you will…' because that makes feeling more relaxed a thing of the future rather than <u>now</u>.

## Tell a story

The first time that you or anybody was hypnotised was when you were told stories as a child. Even to this day you have strong mental images of Little Red Riding Hood and all the characters of fairy tales. What does Rapunzel look like? I bet you have a mental picture from years ago.

We like stories. We relax when we hear descriptions because we have to use our imaginations. The car salesman will talk about how a sports car will feel on a motorway to a young person. The same salesman will talk about driving through a leafy forest to an older prospect. He will talk about pictures of safety to a couple with young children. Same car but different stories. You use the other person's ability to picture, smell and hear in order to get them into a different frame of mind.

When using hypnosis, create a scenario. Get people to imagine being on a beach. Get them to smell the sea, hear the birds and feel the sand. Place them in that crossover world between imagination and memory. Change it to a leafy glade or a riverbank. Like an artist you can then place positive outcomes into those scenes. Get the person to experience a happy and more successful outcome as if it was happening now.

## Ensure relaxation

As obvious as it seems, allow the person to relax. This requires creating a feeling of safety. If you are using hypnosis to mislead or trick somebody for your own gain, forget it. There is a thing called reality checking whereby a compliant person will go along with the story told in the induction. They will become open to positive images for improvements to their lives. However, they will react in the same way as you would if a hairdresser touched you inappropriately. The person you are working with has a threshold of trust. If you step over it, there will be a bad reaction.

## Relaxing somebody

All the techniques that have been described to enable the reader to relax apply here. You need a change in the breathing pattern, deep diaphragmatic breathing brings in the recovery response. Brain wave patterns will change from higher to lower frequencies and this brings about lowered blood pressure and heart rate.

The body posture should be open. The eyes are closed. It is the same as when people drop off to sleep. The language of thought follows the compliant suggestions for relaxation, feelings of safety and security and the mind is absorbed by the story being told.

To put all of the above together, please read through the script in the Stop Smoking chapter. This can be modified to other situations.

## Stage hypnosis

Stage hypnosis is full tricks that are aimed at gaining compliance very quickly. A lot are based on simple, yet effective games played with words and physiology.

The first element is the fact that the person you see on stage is a hypnotist, therefore there is an implied 'power'. This person is assumed to know what they are doing.

Typically, volunteers are called for. By going onto the stage those people have demonstrated the first signs of compliance.

The next part is to get them to clasp their hands together or to link the fingers together and invert them above the head. They are then told that the hands are locked together and that no matter how hard they TRY to pull them apart, they remain clasped together. Notice the use of the word 'try', insinuating failure to do so. The other part, physiology, is that locking the fingers together will starve them of blood and muscle movement is therefore slower. The first hesitation and the failure word get many volunteers to believe they have been controlled.

This belief is strengthened by getting them to believe that their eyelids have been glued together. In order to keep the glue off the eyeballs they are asked to roll the eyes up as if watching a TV screen on the inside of the forehead. They are then told that when they TRY to open the eyes the lids will be firmly stuck together. It is impossible to open the eyes when the eyeballs are rolled up. The same blocks of muscle control the eyelids and the eyeballs. Do it now, but be careful if you wear contact lenses.
Further down the garden path!

The remaining folk on stage will have passed with flying

colours. Those who part their hands or open their eyes are sent back to the audience.

This process continues until enough has been done to convince the people on stage that they really are under the control of the hypnotist.

The imagination is brought to the fore. You can get people to imagine a bag of sugar on one hands and a helium balloon tied to the wrist of the other hand. When the eyes are closed, the imagination will make the hands move slowly as if the situation is real. Or the hands may be turned into magnets and attract each other. After time, the people this is done to will comply through impatience and muscle fatigue.

The act follows.

This can be copied with strangers if you are convincing enough until you ask them to do something that is unacceptable, and if you are reading this to gain advantage over others, these methods never work. However, when your intention is to help, then do so after you are very clear about how to phrase suggestions. Hypnotherapy is best left to trained and experienced therapists.

## Suggestions

In the preceding chapters you have made suggestions for specific problems. Build these into your hypnosis for others always ensuring that they are positive and fit within the compliance of the person you are relaxing. Attempting to influence for your own personal gain is against all principles of hypnotherapy. And it will never work because the person you are dealing with will reject suggestions that they feel unable to accept. Remember that our unconscious mind works for our protection. Inappropriate suggestions will destroy compliance and probably relationships.

## Hypnosis scripts

In the chapter about stopping smoking there is a hypnosis script that can either be used as it is, moderated with different suggestions for other problems or used as a sample upon which you can make your own and different style of script.

The same applies to the script in the Weight Control chapter.

The following chapter explains hypnosis in more detail and will help you to develop your own style.

## CHAPTER EIGHTEEN

## AN EXPLANATION OF HYPNOSIS

## INTRODUCTION AND DEFINITION OF TERMS

**A quick note.** AS MENTIONED EARLIER, whereas the word 'not' is to be avoided in suggestions and self talk dialogue, it is permitted in negating things as shown in the definitions of hypnosis that follow.

**Background.**

As a practising hypnotherapist I have conducted thousands of inductions with a very wide range of people, male and female, covering an age range from 8 to 82, spread widely across the socio-economic spectrum. Therefore a lot of what will be written will be based on my own observations and thoughts, plus widely gathered information from a variety of other material.

**Terminology.**

**'Induction'** refers to the purposeful promotion of hypnosis using a variety of techniques. **'Hypnosis'** is referred to as a condition which is deliberately induced by one person in a compliant other person, or which is wilfully self-induced.

For ease of reading the hypnotised person is referred to as the **'subject'** and the person who induces hypnosis as the **'hypnotist'**.

These terms avoid implying any level of control, nor do they indicate whether hypnosis is being used therapeutically or recreationally. The subject will be referred to as 'he'. The word **'trance'** has a value in defining that a person is exhibiting some, one, or all of the recognisable signs of hypnosis, but unfortunately there is a negative emotional significance in the word suggesting a loss of control and perhaps unconsciousness. This aspect of the word 'trance' should never be assumed, nor should it imply a special and individual state which can only be witnessed or experienced in hypnosis.

The word **'state'** will also be used to signify that the subject is exhibiting some, one, or all of the recognisable signs of hypnosis, rather than a special state that is entered.

In this chapter I will differentiate between inductions and the actual hypnotic 'state'. I take the viewpoint that hypnosis is a naturally occurring phenomenon, and that the concept of a 'state' is used to describe a different frame of mind to 'normal'.

This, of course, requires that a 'normal state' should be defined. This is seemingly impossible to do in a generalised way. For example, a person adding numbers is assumed to be in a 'normal' state of mind, so is an artist painting a picture. However the thinking processes are very different. One is described as 'logical', the other 'creative'.

Hypnosis exists as an observable fact, but it is impossible to define it by a complete and specific series of attributes that have to be present all at once.

**HYPNOSIS AS A PHENOMENON.**

The starting point for explaining how hypnosis works is a definition of what it is.

However before doing so it does seem so much easier to define what hypnosis is not, rather than defining what it is, which is a common feature of the large number of writers on the subject.

**What hypnosis is not.**

The following extracts from 'The Practical Application of Medical and Dental Hypnosis' (1990) seem to best describe the general agreement about what hypnosis is not:

It is not a method to extract secrets.
It does not involve the surrender of will.
It does not mean gullibility.
It does not weaken the mind.
It does not work miracles.
It is not a special power.
It is not unconsciousness.
The subject cannot get stuck in hypnosis.

It is perhaps ironic that whilst publicly agreeing with the above, a large number of hypnotists and hypnotherapists would perhaps disagree with some of those points for the simple reason that the essence of analytical work is to uncover 'repressed' or 'suppressed' memories, secrets, for example, but purely in the context of it being a beneficial confession or 'release'.

The counter argument to this would be the 'compliance' of the subject who agrees to hypnosis and its consequences, which includes the assumption of the ability to facilitate the telling of secrets! Similarly, there would be a consensus of opinion that hypnosis deals with 'unconscious processes', albeit different to the unconscious state.

Therefore, whilst hypnosis will never extract secrets, it does facilitate the release of information that has been locked up but with the agreement of the subject.

I would also add that hypnosis is not necessarily synonymous with relaxation. Although relaxation can usually be observed and experienced during hypnotic inductions, it is often the case that it proceeds to emotional awakening. This can be measured with an electrical skin resistance monitor, and also during aversion therapy, for example, when associating feelings of discomfort with touching a cigarette. Catharsis, the release of pent up emotions attached to events earlier in a client's life, does not evoke a feeling of relaxation, either.

## What hypnosis is.

It is interesting that hypnosis is referred to in the singular rather than in the plural because so many different characteristics are defined that it seems much more likely that there are different conditions which are distinct and unique which are grouped under the single heading of hypnosis, hence there is difficulty in defining 'hypnosis'.

To use an analogy, there are many types of radios, for example the walkie-talkie, transistors, hi-fi's, even mobile telephones. We can define all of them under the generic term 'radio', but the term 'radio' does not define the individual characteristics. Not even all of the characteristics have to be present in order to define an object as a radio.

There is much discussion about whether or not hypnosis is a unique state. A unique state can only be 'proved' if a list all of the individual phenomena which are alleged to be present when a person is 'hypnotised' can be identified, and, if they cannot be perceived when the person is not in hypnosis.

Hypnosis is usually defined by the phenomena which are assumed to be present when a person is in hypnosis, but most of these phenomena are also present in other, 'ordinary' states. These cover two main areas, the subjective and the observable, but I have also added other characteristics which appear to be unique.

**The subjective experiences include (alphabetically):**

**Amnesia** when the subject 'forgets' certain information given by the hypnotist. This can happen spontaneously. When this happens naturally it can be seen as repression or suppression. It might also be more likely that the subject is so relaxed that they have nodded off and they forget what was said when they were asleep.

**Dissociation.** Where different parts of the mind are dissociated as if they were separated. For example dissociation can be used in pain management when the mind seems to be separated from the body and therefore is unable to experience the pain that the body is feeling.

**Logic changes** in which usual logical criteria may be over-ridden, as in the subject being able to communicate with a younger version of himself. This can be witnessed as an increase in the use of imagination, and as such is an important part of the induction process. This may also be experienced as dissociation, in which the subject feels that a part of him is separated, and he feels therefore that he is unable to exert influence or control over actions or feelings.

**Recall** of memories is heightened.

**Recollection** of emotional connections to memories and their release is facilitated.

**Sensory changes** in which the subject can experience sensations unrelated to the environment such as temperature change, heightened perception of the senses such as hearing, anaesthesia, weightlessness, motion, and anxiety. This includes the occurrence of hallucinations in which things are perceived as if they were present when they are not. They can include sights, sounds, smells, tastes, physical sensations and emotional experiences.

Increased **suggestibility** which can sometimes be felt by the subject as surprising, as in for example, arm levitation. Arm levitation is where it is suggested that the arm will float upwards of its own free will. The subject feels that this actually happens when he becomes aware of the arm rising.

**Time distortion** where the perception of time may be accelerated, slowed, or where the subject experiences age regression, in which they feel themselves to be at a different time of life.

### The observable occurrences include (alphabetically):

**Breathing changes** in which the breathing becomes more rapid or slower than the rate at the start of the induction.

**Increase or decrease** in electrical skin resistance (ESR) may be observed if the appropriate measuring device is used.

**Eye movements** where REM, rapid eye movement, and/or eyelid twitching may be seen.

**Heart rate changes** either upward, or more usually downward when measured externally.

**Ideomotor responses** in which a part of the mind seems to control movement which is beyond conscious control. This appears to be a part of dissociation which can be observed and can be allegedly used to communicate without conscious control, such as in finger movement to indicate 'yes' or 'no' answers to questions.

**Muscular changes** in which there may be a tensioning,

catalepsy, or relaxation of muscles which can be seen in bodily alterations as well as in facial symmetry.

**Skin colour changes** where blood flows more easily into relaxed capillaries. This often shows high on the cheeks as a 'hypnotic flush'. This also appears as an indication that the person is in the 'recovery response'.

The observable phenomena which do not appear to be seen in 'natural' functioning include:

**Physical changes.** I have sometimes witnessed the appearance of strangulation marks on the throats of female clients, which have been confirmed as such after a session, and which do not normally show. This can perhaps be proposed to be a natural phenomenon in the same way that blushing is, a social demonstration of something felt but expressed in a physical way. Or perhaps it results from damage to the blood capillaries which becomes apparent when the subject has the normal facial flush described above. (See skin colour changes.)

**Changes in certain reflex actions**, for example the Babinski response in age regressed subjects. This is where the big toe flexes toward to top of the foot and the other toes fan out when the sole of a baby's foot is stroked. This stops when the child becomes reaches infancy. I have not tested this personally but as far as a natural phenomenon is concerned, it occurs at a certain point in life and therefore its occurrence suggests that the response is still present, but repressed, and can be evoked within the relevant framework.

**Depth of trance.**

The concept of depth of trance assumes different stages of hypnosis. The word 'trance' is used in this context as a piece of verbal shorthand, to mean that one, some or all of the signs of hypnosis are present. Depth of trance seems to be an indicator of the presence of other additional signs. In other words, if only some of the indicators are present, the trance is seen as light, but as other indicators become present then the trance is assumed to become deeper.

However, the point may be made that indicators become present in different orders for different people, and that suggestibility tests and the concept of depth of trance may be variable with people of different imagination sub-systems. For example, somebody who finds it difficult to imagine **seeing** the sea and who would therefore be considered to be in a light trance might be able to imagine the **feel** of bobbing up and down on that ocean and would vomit!

I like to think in terms of not so much, depth of trance, but more in terms of width of response, in which a wider range of indicators, independent of each other, becomes apparent, rather than being stacked one on top of the other.

## HOW HYPNOTIC INDUCTIONS WORK

It is not the intention to embark on a discussion of the varieties of individual techniques as used by different hypnotists, but to consider the three basic processes for the creation of hypnotic, or hypnosis-like, 'states' in order to identify the common factors at work.

### 1. Natural situations in which there is no intention to induce hypnosis.

Some examples of naturally occurring aspects of behaviour which resemble hypnosis are:

### Babies in arms
Perhaps the origin of the hypnotic response to soothing sounds and a comfortable and warm place started whilst being suckled. Even the hand movements are replicated

in non-verbal inductions by some therapists who ignore the risks of close physical contact, or near contact, with their subjects.

## Children's' stories
Tales which involve fantasy and imagination told in a safe and comfortable place will encourage a child to enter a 'make-believe' world of strange creatures and situations which are accepted as being real. This is perhaps the basis for the acceptance of metaphors in later life, and early suggestions such as "if you are good, you will grow up to be like Princess Whoever."

## Gypsy/voodoo curses
The suggestion of bad luck or even death can be planted in the mind, and these suggestions are sometimes acted out, even though the logical mind says that they are nonsense.

**Kissing it better.** A basic form of anaesthesia used in childhood where a mother can relieve pain by a simple action and suggestion.

## Out of body experiences
When it is felt that the mind and body are separated. See 'dissociation' in a later section.

## Remembering 'forgotten' words
To a pop song not heard for twenty years. Recall is prompted by clues and cues, and the music, but the active ingredient seems to be the removal of conscious memory searching.

## Seduction
Soft lights, music and softly spoken words in order to suggest a course of action!

## Visualising
A finished room before deciding on decorations. Visualisation is employed in seeing ourselves as we

would like to be and doing what we would like to do.

**Wart charming.**
Warts can be removed by suggestions, perhaps with the rotting of a potato rubbed on the wart and then discarded, a method successfully used by my grandmother on me as a child!

It is possible to infer that people can have a predisposition to enter a different frame of mind, where imagined stimuli are used to simulate real ones. This different frame of mind is where the imagination and remembered experiences are used in order to create a withdrawal from the real world and an acceptance of a fantasised one instead. This was applied in the chapter on flying phobias.

This predisposition was used to great effect by Milton Erickson (1902-1980) who would talk to his patients in such a way that suggestions would be given without recourse to formal inductions. He would use word patterns, metaphors and timing to evoke the frame of mind in which suggestions could, and would, be accepted. There is more on his methodology in a later chapter.

## 2. Purposeful inductions using relaxation as the prime method.

Most relaxation inductions use a mixture of the naturally occurring phenomena listed above in one way or another. A summary of the processes includes environmental settings of:
- Comfortable positioning, either sitting or lying.
- Soft, relaxing music.
- Softly spoken, soothing words.
- A warm environment.

And progressively leading suggestions:
- The directing of different breathing patterns.

166

- Focusing and de-focusing on parts of the body, perhaps with deliberate tensioning and relaxation of muscles.
- Imagining different sights, feelings, smells and sounds.
- Suggestions of mental relaxation and compliance.

The aim of the above is to direct the subject to a position of non-critical acceptance of suggestions intended to:
- Deepen the state
- Encourage beneficial change and/or
- To raise the belief in subjects' abilities to do things which they would normally dismiss as difficult, or impossible, such as recalling memories from a long time ago. For the stage hypnotist this would perhaps include feats of muscular strength, or performing unusual acts in public.

## 3. Shock inductions, conducted either deliberately or naturally.

The first two methods of induction seem to involve three main features, that of imagination, focused attention and compliance (and/or passivity), leading to dissociation from reality. Indeed most inductions seem to involve those approaches, but a third method, that of shock, may also be employed, more often by stage hypnotists and are to be avoided like the plague by serious hypnotherapists and amateurs.

Shock inductions in which sudden movements to produce disorientation, or methods to provoke extremes of fear are used as rapid induction methods by hypnotists who want to work on the illusion of power, although they can be used on subjects who are fearful and who are experiencing the signs of a panic attack. Shock and fear inductions are also those used naturally with and by animals, the classic rabbit frozen in the gaze of a snake.

These rely on the third, seldom mentioned, response within the 'fight-or-flight' situation, that of 'freeze'. Again, these sudden inductions produce dissociation from reality. Perhaps it is better that the rabbit is removed from the impending pain of its oncoming death and consumption! For humans, it may be witnessed in authoritarian situations. A loud shout by a schoolteacher, and a strong suggestion that the pupil is a 'stupid boy' is powerful enough to plant that belief in the mind of a frightened and intimidated person, for example.

This then begs the question, "are states of shock, states of induced relaxation, and naturally occurring suggestibility the same thing?" The answer is that they cannot be, but the linking factor for humans is the heightened receptiveness to dissociation and suggestion, whether positive or negative, internal or external, whether for a change in behaviour or, sometimes, for the recall of memories.

This perhaps explains why the causes of panic attacks and phobias are often very different to the stimuli, as if the current stimulus had mutated. In the state of panic which was felt at the point of cause, the fright reaction was experienced, and the fear of that reaction is transferred to a situation, or object, by the person.

This can be assumed in the case of atavistic phobias (see "Spiders" above), in which the frightening scream of the mother at seeing her daughter playing with a spider, is the real cause of panic, rather than the spider, but, the new stimulus for future fear arousal becomes spiders, rather than the screams. This is possibly a natural response to learn dangers quickly.

**Belief systems.**

The belief system of the subject is important. Without a belief that hypnosis can be induced by the hypnotist, the resistance to opening the mind to suggestions is heightened. On the other hand if there is a belief in the authority and the inference of power in the hypnotist, (whether or not perceived as such, as in the examples of the schoolteacher, snake, priest, doctor, father, etc.), he is much more likely to produce a purposeful, or accidental, induction.

I have noticed that those clients who are referred to me by their doctor, or recommended by a friend, are far more compliant than those who have responded to my advertising. When clients arrive, having been given the suggestion of success by a third party, they are more receptive to the idea of achieving success.

To conclude this section, hypnotic inductions follow naturally occurring processes for bringing about those natural responses. Hypnosis would appear to be an instant learning system for recognising and responding to dangers, as described above as atavistic phobias. Therefore this natural response has a very distinct evolutionary and biological value. The 'hypnotic' responses are present, and the induction processes are also inseparably linked to those responses.

## HOW HYPNOSIS WORKS AS A TOOL

The basis upon which hypnosis is used as a therapeutic tool is that in hypnosis the subject experiences various phenomena which by-pass logical parts of the mind in order to allow acceptance of constructive suggestions to the unconscious mind. Therefore hypnosis can lead to information being processed in a new way that can be used for beneficial modifications.

It is interesting that whilst logic may be by-passed,

thankfully, moral codes cannot. The non-acceptance of suggestions that would endanger the subject, or cause embarrassment, or which would be contrary to the subject's moral code has been well documented.

In the light of the above statement it is interesting to give a brief summary of the principles of various therapeutic practices.

The **psychodynamic model** is based on the idea that there is a conflict between the conscious and unconscious elements of the mind. Therapies attempt to deal with the unconscious causes of that conflict.

**Behavioural therapies** assume that behaviours are conditioned responses to a stimulus. The theory is that behaviours that can be learned can be unlearned, or over-ridden.

**Cognitive therapies** also attempt to develop insight, but into the current thinking processes. The common factor is that cognitive therapies attempt to change the way in which people think about themselves. They include:

**Role-modelling.** Observing the desired behaviour in others is used in the treatment of phobias, for eliminating negative behaviours, and for developing positive behaviours.
**Rational-Emotive Therapy** encourages the client to correct irrational beliefs so that feelings of guilt and self-deprecation can be abolished.
**Cognitive Restructuring Therapy** was developed specifically for the treatment of depression by changing self-defeating assumptions to more positive ones.
**Attributional Therapy** attempts to invert negative beliefs held by depressed people.
**Stress Inoculation Therapy**, attempts to invert negative beliefs held by people suffering with stress.
**Humanistic Therapies** encourage people to consider

themselves in a positive way, and to grow to their full potential.

**Gestalt Therapy** considers emotions and defences but in a guided way, and sometimes in a group situation.

What all the above therapies have in common is the acceptance that there are unconscious causes of problems, and that cause is a direct or indirect stimulus that triggers a response, either physical or emotional.

The key to the resolution of those problems must therefore be assumed to be in the access to the unconscious mind where the beliefs and responses are held. Those problematical beliefs and actions cannot be the result of conscious thoughts, otherwise changing them would be as simple as changing a shirt. The beliefs must be held at a deeper, more fixed level, of the mind as programmes, to use the computer analogy.

Whilst not suggesting that hypnotherapy is a replacement for the above therapies, the point may be made that its direction is similar, if not the same. The thing which helps hypnotherapy is the use of a direct route to the unconscious mind. Once access is gained, changes may be made.

Working on the basis that behaviour, and attitudes are determined by unconscious programming, then changing that behaviour and those attitudes relies on changes to the existing programming. The definitions of hypnosis quoted above revolve around the themes of increased suggestibility, altered states of awareness and/or consciousness, imagination, communication, activation of mental systems, separating channels of mental activity, and the establishment of trains of thought.

In short, they are methods to change the unconscious programming of the mind deliberately. There are also ways in which, perhaps, the mind was mal-programmed in the first place by traumatic events and mistaken behavioural associations, a logical conclusion that seems valid if the proposition that hypnosis is a naturally occurring, and not uncommon, phenomenon.

If this is accepted, then the link to the programming of negative beliefs during moments of shock, emotional trauma, and even 'fiction', can be made. (In order to clarify my use of 'fiction', the reference is made to imagined events and attitudes such as happen in the creation of childhood jealousy, alien abduction, psychosomatic symptoms, etc.).

One of the dilemmas with which I am faced is whether or not to speculate on how the mechanics of changes to unconscious mind are made. Certainly, part of the unconscious mind determines behaviour, attitudes and emotions, and as such is a storehouse of responses to situations. Therefore it seems reasonable to state that the unconscious mind can be changed, although the evidence has to be anecdotal and the mechanisms unclear.

**The different ways in which hypnosis can be used mirror the two main psychotherapeutic approaches.**

The first, reflecting behavioural and cognitive views, is in the use of positive reprogramming to change current beliefs. Techniques would include imagined sensations, (visualising, hearing, feeling, hearing, smelling) future positive outcomes which become new associations which replace the debilitating old responses. For example, a person might be given the feeling of delight at visiting a Department Store, imagining, by suggestion, that she is seeing all the clothes, smelling the perfumes, hearing her children's' laughter in the toy department, etc. rather than experiencing panic attacks at the thought of being out of control.

172

The second, reflecting the psychodynamic approach, is in using the ability to recall previously repressed memories and emotions in order to enable old associations to be examined and therefore discarded in favour of new ones. For example, an older female client might report, after an emotional recall of a forgotten incident: "I am relaxed during a thunder storm. Before, the noise and light reminded me of the horrific times that I had to hide in an air-raid shelter during the War."

The two approaches are not necessarily mutually exclusive. The psychodynamic approach to the first client might be enabling recall to the point when, as a child, she lost sight of her mother whilst shopping one day. The behavioural approach to the second client might be to build on her wish to visit her grandchildren in Florida, where thunder is a regular event.

## CONCLUSIONS

In concluding this chapter and in attempting to give a concise definition of how hypnosis works I present my point of view that "induced hypnosis is a purposeful suggestion of naturally occurring phenomena, amplified by the subject's belief system, and in which a temporary suspension of the subject's logical criteria occurs." Sorry if that sounds a little over the top but it is a good summary even if wordy.

When purposely induced or naturally entered hypnosis, suggestibility increases and the imagination becomes much more powerful. This not only allows the imagination to become more acceptable as a reality, but it also allows new associations to be accepted by the unconscious mind without the interference of the more logical and totally realistic part of the mind.

Hypnosis works because it is a natural condition in which suggestibility is increased, and those suggestions may be either negative or positive, self applied or applied from an outside source.

# CHAPTER NINETEEN

## THE CAUSES OF PANIC, ANXIETY, STRESS AND ANGER IN MORE DETAIL

AN IMPORTANT FACT of life is that we are cave men and women who've been given a very thin veneer of civilisation. That veneer contains our clothing, our use of language and technology and our social rules. However, very close to the surface there's a primeval animal whose biology has remained the same since prehistoric times.

Back in those early days we were vulnerable to attack from other animals and people. Environments were often hostile and posed a threat to our survival.

Whenever a threat arose, the body prepared itself for attack or defence. We developed a 'red alert' state. That response kept our ancestors alive and that is one of the main reasons for us being here today.

But as we now control our environments and we are able to keep potential predators at bay with weapons, that response is inappropriate most of the time, but it lives within us on a hair trigger.

When it happens, adrenaline is released and our muscles are primed for action by blood flowing into them to provide oxygen and energy. When prolonged, another hormone called cortisol is produced which promotes the feelings that are experienced in 'stress'. This reaction is referred to as the 'fight or flight' response. This is what causes panic, anxiety, stress and anger.

The fundamental drive of any animal, including humans, is the survival of the individual. Without survival there cannot be reproduction. In order for a person to survive a life-threatening situation, he or she has to be able to run away from the threat, or fight it in order to gain an advantage. Sometimes, the response is to stay still in the hope that the aggressor will miss noticing him or her and go away.

This response is usually called the **'fight or flight'** response, or the adrenaline rush. Perhaps this should be called the 'fight, run, defend or freeze' response, an altogether more explanatory title. It then becomes easier to understand some reactions that we experience when we are in an anxiety state. The name defines some of the different effects of anxiety. Running and fighting require action, whereas defending and freezing are passive.

**Fighting is** when we can become aggressive and angry. We want to attack the perceived source of our threat. Anger is a reaction to a stimulus that makes us feel vulnerable. Those stimuli may be physical threats or verbal ones. They may be displaced hostile feelings from earlier events in the life of the angry person. Come-what-may, the response is usually inappropriate.

**Running** is where we avoid people and situations. An example of this is the avoidance of people who are dear to us, sometimes the urge to run away from a supermarket queue. The need to escape is overwhelming.

**Defending** is when we become tense, nervous and elusive. We might assign blame to others, or escape into a bottle of whisky in order to give ourselves a mask, which makes us feel different.

**Freezing** is when we feel helpless and unable to act. An example is becoming lethargic or depressed. It could be a desire to stay within the security of our houses, never going out.

The 'fight, run, defend or freeze' response is controlled

by the **autonomic nervous system**, which is beyond our conscious control. We feel the effects such as an increased heart rate. There are two branches of this system. The first is the **'sympathetic nervous system'**. The changes that take place include:

• The production of blood platelets which help the blood to clot in case of injury.
• Our blood flow changes from supplying the skin and digestive system in order to provide muscles with more blood.
• Blood pressure increases.
• Red blood cells are released from the spleen in order to ensure that muscles needed for fighting or running are well provided with oxygen.
• The liver releases sugars to supply energy to the muscles.
• The digestion of food changes. Whereas sugar is metabolised faster to provide energy to the muscles, longer-term digestion is slowed or stopped.
• Other 'long-term' processes are also suppressed, such as the immune system.
• The brain produces endorphins, our natural painkillers.

Those changes are usually unnoticed, but we are aware of others, including:

• Our breathing becoming more rapid to supply more oxygen from the lungs.
• The heart beating faster in order to deliver that extra oxygen to the muscles.
• Sweating increasing to help the body to control the extra heat produced by muscular activity.
• The neck, shoulder and stomach muscles tightening. This is part of our defensive position in order to protect the vulnerable parts of our bodies. For example, predators usually catch their prey by the back of the neck, but we are vulnerable at the fronts of our bodies. The stomach muscles protect the soft organs of the

abdomen. These include the stomach, kidneys, liver and the spleen.
• The awareness of our surroundings is increased, hence the action of staring as if making a threat or the passivity of avoiding looking at people as if signalling submission.

Although panic, anxiety, stress and anger may be defined as separate conditions, the physiological and psychological responses that those conditions evoke are very similar because they are all different manifestations of the fight or flight response.

Briefly, **panic attacks** are an uncontrolled fight-or-flight reaction, hence the word 'panic'. Sufferers will sometimes feel faint, and might feel that they have the symptoms of a heart attack. They might experience dizziness, feelings of choking, and breathing problems. Sometimes there can be problems with feelings of sickness, diarrhoea or incontinence. There might be the urge to escape from or to confront the source of danger.

In contrast to stress and phobias, panic attacks happen at a point in time, rather than being continuous. Panic attacks can happen as a response to a known stimulus, or to an unknown stimulus when they happen 'out-of-the-blue'.

The feeling of panic is a conscious process. The sufferer knows how they feel, and as a result will fear the next attack.

**Anxiety and Stress** are umbrella words. They have many meanings, which depend very much on the context in which they are used. For example, they can be:

• A short-term reaction to particular events.
• Or a long-term reaction.
• Or something that results from situational problems

such as work, social or domestic pressures.

• Or something that results from a series of negative events such as a succession of accidents.

• Or the result of ill health.

However, the main link seems to be the individual's inability to cope with the situation he or she is in.

People who believe that they have control of their own lives have less anxiety and stress than those who believe that they are victims of circumstance.

It can be seen as the fight-or-flight response spread over a much longer period of time. This makes it sinister in that its effects are cumulative and can move toward a crisis point. The feelings of stress will manifest themselves in different ways and the reactions to the feelings of unease will vary.

All life forms seek balance, known as homeostasis. The lion needs to rest after the hunt. The rabbit needs to recover after its escape. Humans need rest and recuperation after struggling with the side-effects of civilisation.

Nature, being perfect, has given us a system, which counteracts the fight or flight response. It's called the **parasympathetic nervous system** and it restores balance. This is what I have referred to as the recovery response.

For example, it reduces the heart rate and blood pressure, restores digestion, stimulates tissue repair and stores sugars as body fats, and much more.

If that could be produced in a pill, it would be referred to as a miracle cure. That miracle is life. We have that system within us. The only thing we have had need of is the key to the cupboard in which it has been locked. That key is in the pages you have read about breathing, posture and language.

The techniques and methods described in this book encourage that wonderful system to operate in order to bring about relaxation, calmness and the elimination of the panic response, anxiety, stress and anger, as well as many other anxiety related problems.

# CHAPTER TWENTY

## GOAL ACHIEVEMENT AND VISUALISATION

THERE IS MORE to goal achievement than making goals. That is the first step. It then becomes necessary to work towards them.

If I want to be a great musician and I am unable to play any instruments or sing then I have to learn. If you want to be a successful business person then you have to know what you are doing.

However, that first step is essential to getting or doing what you want. The goal is the outcome of everything you do and the way in which you do it. It may be that you are a great inventor but you are unable to sell your product. Being a better inventor is unnecessary; you need to be a better sales person.

As mentioned earlier, the greatest antidote to worry is hope, the last thing out of Pandora's Box. In Greek mythology, Pandora's Box was in fact was a jar that contained negative things such as plague, poverty, crime, greed, old age and sickness. It also contained negative emotions such as sorrow, despair, spite, passion and so on. Pandora was given the jar and told not to open it (negative suggestion!) but her curiosity got the better of her and she opened it letting all those strange things out to spoil the joy of mankind. She closed the lid quickly leaving just one more thing inside.

Luckily for us, Pandora later opened the jar one more time and **hope** flew out so that in times of adversity there is always that positive thing on our side.

That metaphorical story is what we have to remember. When we need to achieve something then we define our goals and the vision of our achievement is that essence of hope that motivates us to apply ourselves to reaching our destination.

In goal setting there are no limits. Every successful person on this planet who was born without a silver spoon is, and was, the same as you. If you feel that you lack their attributes then borrow them by way of role modelling. That is, act as they did and do. You are unable to fly in a private jet but if you set that as a goal you know that you have to work as hard as the people who own them. You need to apply yourself to your achievement.

Let us take different examples to those of becoming very rich.

If you want to meet and talk to other people but you are shy, watch good conversationalists and copy what they do and how they do it. See how they hold their bodies, their faces and how they move to others to start talking. You will notice that seemingly good talkers are actually very good at asking questions and then listening to the answers. They lead talk rather than make talk. Examples are:

"How are you?"
"What do you do for a living?"
"What are your hobbies?"
"What do you think about the headlines?"

These are leading questions that need an explanatory answer rather than simple questions such as "Do you like opera?" that require nothing more than a 'yes' or 'no' answer.

**What's in it for me?**

Develop empathy. Put yourself inside the other person's head. Ask yourself how much they understand about what you talking about. Our inventor above will never sell his product if he starts a sales pitch with, "I have invented a triptosquiggulator and I think it would be a good product for you." The person he is talking to wants to know what the product will do for him. So our inventor should start, "I have developed a product that will minimise your needs for electricity and will save you millions of pounds in your production costs." Now he has interest. "So how does it work?" is the reply. "It triptosquiggulates the solar energy that falls onto you factory roof and converts it to electricity. It is environmentally friendly and so on and so on."

Selling benefits is more than something that is used for products. "I would like a job in your company, please." Says nothing. "I am a person with experience of making profits in your industry and I am able to apply those skills instantly." Gets interest. The guy you are talking to is more interested in increasing his profits rather than you as a human being. Once he realises that you are able to benefit him, then he is interested in you.

Write down your benefits to other people, to businesses, to the arts, to person-kind and whichever other categories you can. I know already that you will hit walls. "I am of no use to anybody!" Oh yes you are. Start again and again until you have a big list. Copy the attributes of others, find similarities. Hey, celebrities have little use other than being celebrities. So why do we have them? They must have some use, surely!

So what does this achieve? It increases your feeling of self worth. It builds confidence. People who lack confidence need to discover the gems that they are that are covered in dirt. That is you. Find your inner qualities and resources.

**Role modelling**

Write down the name of somebody who you think is better at achieving things than you, or how you would like to be in the space below and then write what you

182

notice about them. If you find it difficult to remember then make a note next time you see them.

| Name of role model: | |
|---|---|
| **How they are:** | **Describe their features:** |
| How they stand? | |
| How do they sit? | |
| How they look? | |
| How they speak? | |
| Where do they look? | |
| How do they react? | |
| Their body language | |
| Their clothes | |
| Their hair | |

Now copy them. Rather than stealing something you are paying them a compliment.

If your goal is to become as successful, in whichever field, then become so much like them that it becomes natural. This is method acting, wearing a mask that is fitting for the part. Dustin Hoffman lived the life of an autistic person for his role in Rain Man. He never became autistic but he copied the idiosyncrasies to perfection.

Be assertive (rather than aggressive). Compare "Do you have a reservation for me for dinner, please? My name is Jones." with "Hello. My name is Jones. You have a reservation for me this evening." Said to a restaurant waiter the second makes a statement rather than asking a question that requires a 'yes' or 'no' answer. If the restaurant is overbooked then you will lose it in the first instance and get in the second. Build assertion into your speech to avoid people taking advantage of you.

So, set your goals, develop the skills and the role model to achieve them. Find your personal assets and build on them. Just go for it but make sure it is legal!

# CHAPTER TWENTY ONE

## MILTON ERICKSON

THE MAN WHO TOOK hypnotherapy from a Cinderella therapy to a proper and respectable occupation was Milton Erickson. This chapter describes his work and contributions and helps us all to understand the use of the secret languages of hypnotherapy much better.

The main medium in most hypnotic situations is the spoken word, and one of the greatest contributions that Erickson made to hypnosis is in the use of words and language. Hypnosis, to Erickson, was very much about communication.

### 1. Language

He used language and words in a creative way in order to bring about changes in a very subtle way. He was dyslexic which probably accounts for his different comprehension and understanding of language and the nuances of meaning. As a result of his dyslexia and his fairly basic schooling in a very rural environment, he learnt to view words and their shape in different ways to others.

He relates the story about his debating coach using a creative method to help him to read and pronounce the word 'government' by inserting the name of a fellow student, 'La Verne', in the middle, and omitting the 'La'. This principle of using the unexpected in order to change perspective and thereby facilitate change extended to his whole approach to the use of therapeutic hypnosis, and might even be taken as a very precise summary of the concept of lateral thinking, as later developed by Edward de Bono.

Not only did he use the pattern of breaking words up as in the preceding example, he would also break sentences up into 'sub-sentences' in order to covertly convey their intrinsic meanings. He did this by inflection and timing. Using an example, the sentence, 'As you *breathe gently*, and as you *continue to relax* to the sound of my voice...' may be broken into the instructions which are shown in italics, their direct meaning being given by a change in voice tone or volume. Thereby, firm commands are presented in a very mild way, which do not provoke hostility or counter-action.

Furthermore, the use of the word 'as' gives the impression that different actions are linked in a conditional way, which is not necessarily the case. The above sentence implies that the patient will continue to listen to the therapist rather than do something else like think about last night's television programme.

His special use of language extends to the use of the **double bind**. He approached problems in a very creative way, sometimes by appearing to ask the person to do the opposite to what had been assumed. The double bind is the apparent choice between two options, either of which will achieve the desired result. The start of Erickson's use of the double bind is credited to a time in his early childhood when his father challenged him to pull a stubborn calf into a barn. Instead of pulling its head, the young Erickson pulled its tail, so that the calf had two choices, either to resist the weaker pull on the tail or to give way to the stronger pull on the head. It chose the pull on the head and moved into the barn.

This was developed and the principle used later when working with hypnosis. For example, a desired but hidden outcome is embedded within a choice, such as 'you can either go into a light or a deep trance'. This overtly states that the person can choose which level to go into, but the assumption that is accepted by the person is that they will go into trance, the intended outcome.

## 2. Stories.

He used **anecdotes, metaphors, analogies** and **humour** in order to emphasise a desired outcome in a way which was less obvious to a conscious critical interpretation, whilst allowing the true meaning of his stories to be taken into the unconscious mind.

Erickson had a sense of humour, probably developed as a defence mechanism when he was younger. He would have seemed different to many other people as a result of his illnesses and problems. In later life he was able to use humour, anecdotes from his life, and metaphors in order to communicate in a more effective way than straightforward speech, and to establish a relationship of mutual co-operation rather than one of the authority of the expert.

The books titled 'Seminars, Workshops and Lectures of Milton H. Erickson' by Milton H. Erickson, Ernest L. Rossi, and Florence A. Sharp are well illustrated with his stories in order to explain points (in much the same way as he would have used stories with his patients) and are essential reading for any serious student of hypnotherapy. The stories are about his own life and family as well as about patients, and are used in an illustrative way. One of the key factors in his use of anecdotes, analogies, metaphors and humour is that they relate directly to the patient. The following examples illustrate that point. When treating a young child who could not use the school lavatory, Erickson discovered that the boy had an interest in spaceships. Erickson focused on that interest in space travel and gently moved the story into the need to use a lavatory in a public situation, as space flight would be. The child recognised his own need to overcome his problem at some stage in his life.

Had Erickson used an authoritative approach, or an analogy with something outside the child's interest, the results would have been lessened because the child would not have related so much to the beneficial outcome for himself, and might even have resisted the help as he had apparently done so before. Many people must have told him that he 'must go' (to the lavatory) in the past.

In the other example, Erickson uses a story about a doctor who unknowingly developed a post-hypnotic amnesia. This was told to a delegate at a seminar as part of a story about eating a meal and forgetting about it afterwards. Again, the story reflected the circumstances of the subject, he was either a dentist or a doctor, and therefore Erickson demonstrated that doctors can be influenced to do things against their own rational understanding of what was happening. Had Erickson used a story about a schoolgirl, the relevance of his desired results to his subject would have been less marked, and therefore less effective, I presume.

## 3. Non-Verbal Communication

Communication also includes non-verbal communication. After his first bout of polio at the age of seventeen, Erickson was virtually completely paralysed. During his recovery of movement, he was very aware of small movements of his muscles, relying to a great extent upon 'muscle memories', remembering how he used to move his fingers, for example. He used those memories of muscle movements in order to stimulate his sensory-motor co-ordination.

Therefore, to a huge extent, his recovery of movement was a result of his own self-exploration. Even when small movements were difficult to make by conscious will, the barely noticeable movements that he obtained were significant to him. He considered each individual to have the strengths, **'dormant resources'** to overcome their own problems, but there was a need to have a method to elicit those resources.

As a result of his own self-recovery he developed an awareness of small movements which would be beyond the normal observation of others who had not been made so sensitive to them.

This recognition of small unconscious movements is the essence of **body language**, non-verbal communication, which is mostly taken for granted. However, when in Erickson's situation of isolated paralysis, any communication to him, or by him, would have taken on a tremendous significance far beyond that of 'normal' communication.

He used **body language**, unconscious communication, at different levels. This could be by the use of small unconscious movements, or by subtle movements of, for example, the head to show disagreement when the conscious response was one of agreement.

He also used **'ideomotor signalling'** in a similar way, but as a direct response to questions. The patient was asked to make a response directly from the unconscious mind by moving a part of the body, typically a finger, as a 'yes' or 'no' answer to a question. Although the verbal answer might be one thing, the ideomotor response could indicate a totally different one.

## 4. Inductions.

Erickson considered inductions of hypnosis as a means to an end. They were less important than the 'state' of hypnosis in which constructive work could be done. Therefore there are no set induction methods but he demonstrated versatility in his approach. As a creative thinker, Erickson could be flexible in his approaches to patients.

His inductions varied from more formal and recognisable ones to those which were more suitable to the patients' circumstances. Therefore if Erickson considered it better to disguise his approach in order to be more effective, then he would. After all, his aim was to help the patient, not to prove that he could hypnotise people. With this approach he demonstrated his empathetic nature.

He seemed to avoid rigid methods of induction, preferring to make the induction part of the natural flow of his sessions. His treatment started at the beginning of a session rather than as something that commenced after the formal induction process.

To use a descriptive phrase from American business, 'he hit the runway with the wheels spinning', rather than performing the induction, and then moving to the main purpose.

His styles of induction gathered many different descriptive names. The following are examples of some of them, including **naturalistic, permissive, confusion and indirect.**

The **naturalistic** induction happens as a naturally occurring response within the therapeutic relationship between therapist and client, the therapist following the leads given by the client and vice versa.

His **permissive** approach was basically the opposite of the authoritarian approach. Although that sounds remarkably obvious it was a fundamental change in the use of hypnosis prior to Erickson. The approach basically involved asking the patient to do things rather than demanding that the patient does things.

An example of the use of the **confusion** technique will illustrate the point. Erickson is sets up irrefutable propositions that in other words say, "No matter what you think, you are going into hypnosis, and furthermore, if you start to think otherwise with your conscious mind then that is a good indication that you are going into hypnosis, so I will let you think what you like rather than telling you what to do, but the outcome will be that you will go into hypnosis". This is very similar to the double bind.

The **indirect** approach to induction and suggestion is exactly as it sounds. Suggestions are paraphrased to appear to be something different which is agreeable to the patient. When the patient comprehends the true meaning of the example or metaphor, then the appropriate meaning for that patient can be assimilated. This is used when there is resistance to accepting ideas.

## TECHNIQUES

### 1. Role Modelling.

Role modelling is an extension of the use of analogies to situations where different action and behaviour are considered to be desirable. In order to learn to walk again, he used his younger sister as a 'role-model'. He watched her own attempts to learn to walk. He observed her patterns so that he could copy them in his mind, and with his own body. Not only did this help him to be able to walk again, it made him an attentive spectator of people, looking not only for obvious signs but needing to be aware of the tiny nuances of actions.

### 2. 'inner natural resources'.

When Erickson used the 'inner natural resources' he was presenting ideas that fitted with the patient's belief system. In this way the new ideas could be accepted, but if ideas which were alien to the patient were presented, there was a high probability of rejection.

Examples are given in the part of this chapter which considers pain control. If a person is hurting, he knows that he is hurting, and telling him that he is not, is an unacceptable concept. However, to tell him that he can remember, initially, a small amount of comfort is acceptable

To use my own analogy, the process is similar to the process used in Judo, when a person pushes, it is better to pull him, using his own strength rather than to push him back. This uses his resources instead of creating resistance

This becomes part of the explanation for the success of using metaphors and analogies.

### 3. Reality Orientation.

Reality orientation refers to the relationship that the patient has to the external world, whether real or imaginary. In an ordinary waking state the reality orientation is continually checked by reference to external cues. In hypnosis however, the reality orientation focuses inwards, so that external stimuli are less important, and the reality orientation becomes based on internal thoughts, suggestions and imaginings. It becomes fixed unless major changes take place.

This becomes the reasoning behind phenomena such as dissociation when used in pain control. The patient might be told to watch the television while the body remains in bed. The reality orientation is set up so that the patient can accept the concept of being in his lounge, using memories as the basis for that reality.

### 4. Reframing.

Reframing is the process of looking at a behaviour or belief from a different point of view, and by so doing, changing its effects.

Erickson's use of this method for the treatment for premature ejaculation is appropriate for describing reframing. In this case a man who suffered from premature ejaculation was given the idea that sooner or later he would suffer the opposite condition, that of failure to ejaculate for at least 27 minutes. The man's problem was reframed to a new problem, that of ejaculation failure which was enough to worry the man so that he forgot about his anxieties concerning the possibility of premature ejaculation. You might recognise the method from earlier in this book.

## 5. Pain Control.

During his recovery from polio he became skilful at controlling pain. Later in his life it enabled him to understand and control the pain of others as well as his own recurring pain. His own sufferings obviously gave him enormous empathy in addition to heightened credibility in using pain control techniques.

His physical disabilities gave a very visible proof that he knew what he was dealing with. He was aware that pain was a complex thing; it was felt in different ways and in different time scales. There are remembered and anticipated pains in addition to the current pain and time distortion, a feature of hypnosis. Therefore hypnosis could be utilised to constructively change the cognition of pain. Thus frequencies and durations of painful episodes could be changed.

The following summarises the techniques for pain control that he outlined in his lectures:

•   **Analgesia**, absence of pain, can be produced locally by hypnosis. Erickson preferred this to anaesthesia, the loss of sensibility, because he felt that the patient should be aware of other senses but be free of pain.
•   **Disorientation** so that the patient becomes confused about which part of the body the pain is supposed to be in.
•   **Displacement.** He also displaced pain by re-interpreting it so that the mind became bored with the tedium of defining the type of pain and its exact

location, and eventually stopped remembering that there was pain. He used displacement of pain from a very sensitive part of the body to a 'less important' part, for example, pain in the whole body to a foot or a hand.

• **Dissociation,** the imagined removal of the mind from the body containing the pain. He would suggest that patients could move, in their minds, to a different place such as watching television or sitting in a garden, while the body that held the pain would remain in the hospital bed.

• **Fractionally diminishing pain** by suggesting that small losses of pain would not be noticeable, so that eventually the patient would agree and accept the sum of those small losses adding up to a large loss.

• **Memory of comfort before pain.** Rather than thinking about pain, patients were asked to recall prior feelings of comfort. The concentration on those feelings of comfort would displace the feelings of pain.

• **Sensations of pain** are broken down into smaller parts in order to give focus to specific sensations that could be dealt with more effectively than trying to treat a broader and more vague condition.

## HIS THEORIES

This heading is written in an ironic way because he was fairly disinterested in theorising about his processes. Erickson was a practical man who was happy to know that something worked.

However, the real basis of Erickson's work is his belief in the enormous power of the **unconscious mind**. These beliefs came not only from his personal experiences, but also from his observation of changes in his patients.

His personal experiences extended beyond his battles against the effects of his illness and disabilities. He relates a story of how he wrote editorials for a local newspaper during the night by programming himself to type at night without conscious awareness. He viewed the unconscious mind as a storehouse of experience and knowledge that had been gained during the life of the individual. That store of experience could be utilised therapeutically.

Erickson considered hypnosis, when used correctly, to be a very effective way to access that reserve of experience.

**CONCLUSIONS**

In order to summarise Erickson's contributions it is necessary to consider him a person, a creative practitioner and an advocate of a new approach to the subject. He possessed empathy, probably as a result of his own problems and pain in his early, and later, life.

Therefore he treated people as unique individuals rather than as stereotypes of a generalised human model. He must certainly have been a strong man to gain the respect and admiration of his peers and by so doing gave credibility to what had been hitherto perceived as an eccentric method of treatment. His creativity of thinking allowed him to develop the many techniques and practices outlined above, that were tailored to a wide range of needs. It is difficult to speculate about how hypnotherapy would have developed without the influence of Erickson, but it is probably safe to assume that it would not have been as well developed as it is now, and perhaps the spin-off interests of things like NLP would not have happened.

This new direction allowed the needs and desires of the patient to be fulfilled through techniques of hypnosis rather than the patient being treated through the assumed 'power' of the hypnotist. Erickson changed the direction of hypnosis to a forward looking and positive one. He added humanity and dignity which legitimised a hitherto misunderstood technique.

# CHAPTER TWENTY TWO

## PARTING COMMENTS

Hypnosis and hypnotherapy are all about communication. At one level the therapist communicates with the client. At the next level the therapist, or the individual, is in contact with the unconscious mind. There are languages that are effective and others where words and thoughts are misheard or misunderstood. This book shows you how to talk to your mind using language, breathing, body posture and body systems that are little understood.

My hope is that you have been able to learn things of value to enhance your life and the lives of others.

**A note of caution.**

With my explanations I hope I have deterred to a great extent, the amateur who wishes to apply do-it-yourself hypnotherapy to his family or friends for fun. I have been asked how long it took me to learn how to hypnotise people. The answer I give is, "About five minutes. Learning how to use it correctly took years and years."

Please remember that hypnosis is a valuable tool but it is one that should be used responsibly and carefully. Far from being a party game, it is as powerful as an influence. In using it NEVER run the risk of hurting others by being reckless.

# CHAPTER TWENTY THREE

## FURTHER HELP

THERE ARE MANY THINGS that I am unable to cover in this book because they are beyond the scope of self help. Things such as abuse, trauma recovery, serious eating disorders, marital problems and domestic violence.

For these problems the first course of action is to seek the appropriate help from doctors, therapists and counsellors.

As this book will be around for a while I suggest that you visit my website for more information. The address is

### http://www.hypnofleet.co.uk

I am unable to answer questions about individual problems by email. However, if you wish to email me on any of the issues raised in the book you will find me at:

### smale@hypnofleet.co.uk

Please put into the subject line the title '**hypnotherapy question**' in order to help me to avoid spam.

**Other publications by the author include:**

BOOKS
**The Secret Language of Hypnotherapy**
**ISBN:** 978-0-9550736-2-5

**Mind Changing Short Stories and Metaphors**
**ISBN:** 978-0-9550736-4-9

**Short Stories and Metaphors**
**ISBN:** 978-0-9550736-3-2

AUDIO
**Insight to Anger**
Metaphorical stories about the destructive nature of anger and how anger can be overcome.

**Stop Smoking**
How to stop smoking easily and safely using hypnosis and breathing techniques.

**Weight Control**
How to reshape your body using hypnosis and visualisation. This method has helped thousands of people.

**Fantasies and Dreams**
Relaxation and positive thinking.

**Self-Hypnosis**
How to relax, visualise and set positive suggestions for yourself.

**Animal Nature**
Metaphors that relax and change the way you think based on animal stories.

**Human Nature**
Metaphors that relax and change the way you think based on stories about people.

**Nature's Nature**
Metaphors that relax and change the way you think based on stories from nature.

More information from:
**http://www.emp3books.com**

SEP 2 2 2009

LaVergne, TN USA
03 September 2009

156925LV00002B/9/P